PRAISE FOR *YOU WERE MADE FOR THIS MOMENT*

"The last few years have seemed like a never-ending bitter winter. We've experienced a global pandemic, political chaos, riots, economic recession, and much more. In times like these, we need an experienced guide to help us. I can think of no one better than my friend Max to lead us to springtime. The words that flow from his pen are good medicine for our souls. Lean into this book and let God's grace lean into you."

> —Dr. Derwin L. Gray, cofounder and lead pastor of
> Transformation Church; author of *God, Do You Hear
> Me? Discovering the Prayer God Always Answers*

"In *You Were Made for This Moment*, Max masterfully brings to life the power of the book of Esther and its relevance to our lives today. This profound message of hope and courage is one we urgently need as we navigate the challenges of living in this chaotic world. We are reminded that impossible is where God starts, and miracles are what God does. I didn't want this book to end and neither will you."

> —Christine Caine, cofounder of A21 and Propel Women

"Max Lucado is one of the best authors alive at bringing the Bible to life. By effortlessly weaving practical teaching and modern-day experiences into the ancient text of the Bible, Max places you in the middle of biblical times as if you were living alongside the characters themselves. The story of Esther has always been intriguing and compelling to me. A true underdog, Esther believed God for the impossible and changed history with her faith. Get ready for an inspiring, uplifting, and faith-building experience in Max Lucado's new book, *You Were Made for This Moment*."

> —Craig Groeschel, pastor of Life.Church and
> *New York Times* bestselling author

"This book hit me to the core as a Christian and a Black woman. I've read the book of Esther so many times, I've even had people use Esther 4:14 to describe my career, but Max took us on a journey that only he could by providing a fresh new lens to this ancient story. Max weaves in and out of the story of Esther with modern-day stories that remind the reader of God's presence when we feel forgotten; our habit of focusing on what we can lose instead of what we can gain by standing up for what is right; and the importance of not running away from 'Mordecai moments.' Thank you, Max!"

—Maggie John, TV anchor/ producer of *Context Beyond the Headlines* and former host of *100 Huntley Street*

"I have long admired Max Lucado as an author whose writings are full of encouragement, hope, and love—with stories that touch the hearts of all ages."

—Nicky Gumbel, vicar of Holy Trinity Brompton and pioneer of Alpha

"For those of us who have ever believed the lie that God can no longer use us to make a difference, Max proclaims: 'You were made for this moment. You. Me. Us. We.' Through rich biblical insights and compelling storytelling, discover how God invites us to participate in his holy work and uses our experiences and circumstances to bless more people than we can imagine. That's an adventure I want to be a part of. Join me."

—Amy Grant, Grammy Award–winning recording artist

"*You Were Made for This Moment* was written at the right place and the right time. I have struggled with the lows that Max writes about and experienced firsthand that 'today's confusion and crisis will be tomorrow's conquest.' Max's theme for this book reminds me of the first song I wrote after becoming a Christian titled, 'The Struggle.' His call to recast *your* struggle as an opportunity for God to resurrect life out of death is just what our brothers and sisters need right now. Thank you, Max, for once again reminding us that no struggle is too hard for God."

—Zach Williams, multiple Grammy and Dove Award–winning recording artist

"We will all face seasons that seem overwhelming, times of unexpected and undeserved troubles that give rise to fear and intimidate us. In his powerful new book, *You Were Made for This Moment*, my dear friend Max Lucado uses the courageous story of Esther to not only encourage each of us as we face these 'Arctic winters' but to show us that God has placed inside of us the will and determination to achieve our divine destiny when we trust in him."

—Victoria Osteen, copastor Lakewood Church

"Even the strongest of leaders have seasons of winter that can break us: the world is dark, the day is lonely, and God is silent. And yet, as Max Lucado explains with such empathy and encouragement, they are also the moments that can make us. *You Were Made for This Moment* will change the way you look at the challenges in your life—there is purpose in the pain and opportunity in the opposition."

—Kadi Cole, leadership consultant, executive coach, and author of *Developing Female Leaders*, www.kadicole.com

"If you've ever felt like God has vacated the world, your life, or both, you'll love *You Were Made for This Moment*. In a way only Max Lucado can, Max makes a biblical story jump off the page and speak freshly directly into the bleakness that too often feels like today. Just when you were about to give up, you'll not only find God, you'll also find your role in the story."

—Carey Nieuwhof, author of *At Your Best*, podcaster and speaker

"Boldly confronting the reality of crises in our world today, and the challenge of living out faith in a faithless society, *You Were Made for This Moment* is a gift to all of us still finding our way. Well-researched, refreshing, witty, and full of personal, thoughtful insights, Max weaves an old story into a fresh narrative, perfectly matching the book of Esther with our current struggles."

—Bruxy Cavey, teaching pastor at the Meeting House and author of *The End of Religion*

"Max continues in his tradition of brilliant storytelling as he captures the story of Esther. This is a story for now and for such a time as this, in our present day. This book demonstrates the relevance of the story of Esther and how our struggle is often our strength. Our challenges can be used to shape a generation if our view of God remains larger than ourselves."

—Latasha Morrison, founder and president of Be the Bridge

"You were made for this moment! You are God's person! Regardless of where you've been and what you've done, Max Lucado invites us on a courageous journey to follow God's call even when we feel unqualified and especially when we deem ourselves unready."

—Paula Faris, host of *The Paula Faris Faith and Calling Podcast*, author, speaker

ALSO BY MAX LUCADO

INSPIRATIONAL

3:16
A Gentle Thunder
A Love Worth Giving
And the Angels Were Silent
Anxious for Nothing
Because of Bethlehem
Before Amen
Come Thirsty
Cure for the Common Life
Facing Your Giants
Fearless
Glory Days
God Came Near
Grace
Great Day Every Day
He Chose the Nails
He Still Moves Stones
How Happiness Happens
In the Eye of the Storm
In the Grip of Grace
It's Not About Me
Just Like Jesus
Max on Life
More to Your Story
Next Door Savior
No Wonder They Call
 Him the Savior
On the Anvil
Outlive Your Life
Six Hours One Friday
The Applause of Heaven
The Great House of God
Traveling Light
Unshakable Hope
When Christ Comes
When God Whispers
 Your Name
You Are Never Alone
You'll Get Through This

COMPILATIONS

Begin Again
Jesus

FICTION

Christmas Stories
Miracle at the Higher
 Grounds Café
The Christmas Candle

BIBLES (GENERAL EDITOR)

The Lucado Encouraging
 Word Bible
Children's Daily
 Devotional Bible
Grace for the Moment
 Daily Bible
The Lucado Life
 Lessons Study Bible

CHILDREN'S BOOKS

A Max Lucado
 Children's Treasury
Do You Know I
 Love You, God?
God Always Keeps
 His Promises
God Forgives Me,
 and I Forgive You
God Listens
 When I Pray
Grace for the Moment:
 365 Devotions for Kids
Hermie, a Common
 Caterpillar
I'm Not a Scaredy Cat
Itsy Bitsy Christmas
Just in Case You
 Ever Wonder

Lucado Treasury of
 Bedtime Prayers
One Hand, Two Hands
Thank You, God,
 for Blessing Me
Thank You, God,
 for Loving Me
The Boy and the Ocean
The Crippled Lamb
The Oak Inside the Acorn
The Tallest of Smalls
You Are Mine
You Are Special
Where'd My Giggle Go?

YOUNG ADULT BOOKS

3:16
It's Not About Me
Make Every Day Count
Wild Grace
You Were Made to
 Make a Difference

GIFT BOOKS

Fear Not Promise Book
For the Tough Times
God Thinks You're
 Wonderful
Grace for the Moment
Grace Happens Here
Happy Today
His Name Is Jesus
Let the Journey Begin
Live Loved
Mocha with Max
Safe in the Shepherd's
 Arms
This Is Love
You Changed My Life

You Were
MADE FOR THIS
MOMENT

COURAGE FOR TODAY AND HOPE FOR TOMORROW

MAX LUCADO

THOMAS NELSON

Since 1798

Published in Nashville, Tennessee, by Thomas Nelson. Thomas Nelson is a registered trademark of HarperCollins Christian Publishing, Inc.

Thomas Nelson titles may be purchased in bulk for educational, business, fundraising, or sales promotional use. For information, please email SpecialMarkets@ThomasNelson.com.

Any Internet addresses, phone numbers, or company or product information printed in this book are offered as a resource and are not intended in any way to be or to imply an endorsement by Thomas Nelson, nor does Thomas Nelson vouch for the existence, content, or services of these sites, phone numbers, companies, or products beyond the life of this book.

Unless otherwise noted, Scripture quotations are taken from the Holy Bible, New International Version®, NIV®. Copyright © 1973, 1978, 1984, 2011 by Biblica, Inc.® Used by permission of Zondervan. All rights reserved worldwide. www.zondervan.com. The "NIV" and "New International Version" are trademarks registered in the United States Patent and Trademark Office by Biblica, Inc.®

Scripture quotations marked BSB are from the Holy Bible, Berean Study Bible, BSB. Copyright © 2016, 2018 by Bible Hub. Used by permission. All rights reserved worldwide. Scripture quotations marked ESV are from the ESV® Bible (The Holy Bible, English Standard Version®). Copyright © 2001 by Crossway, a publishing ministry of Good News Publishers. Used by permission. All rights reserved. Scripture quotations marked GW are from God's Word®. © 1995, 2003, 2013, 2014, 2019, 2020 by God's Word to the Nations Mission Society. Used by permission. Scripture quotations marked KJV are from the King James Version. Scripture quotations marked THE MESSAGE are from *The Message*. Copyright © 1993, 2002, 2018 by Eugene H. Peterson. Used by permission of NavPress. All rights reserved. Represented by Tyndale House Publishers, a Division of Tyndale House Ministries. Scripture quotations marked NASB are from the New American Standard Bible®. Copyright © 1960, 1962, 1963, 1968, 1971, 1972, 1973, 1975, 1977, 1995 by The Lockman Foundation. Used by permission. www.Lockman.org. Scripture quotations marked NCV are from the New Century Version®. Copyright © 2005 by Thomas Nelson. Used by permission. All rights reserved. Scripture quotations marked NKJV are taken from the New King James Version®. Copyright © 1982 by Thomas Nelson. Used by permission. All rights reserved. Scripture quotations marked NLT are from the Holy Bible, New Living Translation. Copyright © 1996, 2004, 2015 by Tyndale House Foundation. Used by permission of Tyndale House Ministries, Carol Stream, Illinois 60188. All rights reserved. Scripture quotations marked PHILLIPS are from the New Testament in Modern English by J. B. Phillips. Copyright © 1960, 1972 J. B. Phillips. Administered by The Archbishops' Council of the Church of England. Used by permission. Scripture quotations marked TLB are from The Living Bible. Copyright © 1971. Used by permission of Tyndale House Publishers, a Division of Tyndale House Ministries, Carol Stream, Illinois 60188. All rights reserved.

ISBN 978-1-4002-3180-5 (eBook)
ISBN 978-1-4002-3179-9 (HC)
ISBN 978-1-4002-3186-7 (IE)

Library of Congress Control Number: 2021942662

Printed in the United States of America

21 22 23 24 25 LSC 10 9 8 7 6 5 4 3 2 1

To our precious friend, Margaret Bishop.
An Esther of your generation, you model courage,
faith, and beauty. Denalyn and I are honored to know
you and thrilled to grandparent alongside you.

CONTENTS

ACKNOWLEDGMENTS

Once upon a time, in a moment before moments existed, two angels were reviewing the job description of a yet-to-be-born fellow named Max. The assignment said: *writer of Christian books*. Yet, when the angels saw the skill set of Max and the responsibility of an author, one angel said, "We need to take this up the chain of command. Lucado ain't got what it takes to do this job." The other angel replied, "I don't like your grammar, but agree with your concern."

So, they sought an explanation. Here is what they were told. "You are correct. Lucado is going to need all the help heaven can muster. As a result, the following team members are assigned to keep him afloat:

- Liz Heaney and Karen Hill—editors of exceptional skill. They could prod a donkey to dance and teach a fish to sing.
- Carol Bartley—she is so capable, that we plan to ask her to copy edit the Book of Life for typos.
- David Drury—had he been born two thousand years earlier, he would have been on epistle duty. He will keep Lucado on the doctrinal straight and narrow.

- Steve and Cheryl Green—everyone needs friends like Steve and Cheryl. We reserved them for Max.
- The HCCP team of heroes—Mark Schoenwald, Don Jacobson, Tim Paulson, Mark Glesne, Erica Smith, Janene MacIvor, and Laura Minchew. There's enough talent on that team to run a galaxy.
- Greg and Susan Ligon—they are receiving twice the quota of spiritual gifts. They will lead, serve, administer, encourage, and counsel. Superstars, they are!
- Dave Treat—he prays like Daniel and looks like Moses.
- Peggy Campbell, Jim Sanders, and the Ambassador team— they are set apart from on high to shepherd dozens of spiritual shepherds. They will treat Lucado with loving care.
- Caroline Green—the perfect Martha/Mary combination. A go-getter and a Jesus-lover.
- Andrea Lucado—same last name, but far smarter than her dad.
- Jana Muntsinger and Pamela McClure—a rare blend of smile and savvy; perfect for publicity.
- Janie Padilla and Margaret Mechinus—ever steady, quiet, and rock solid.
- Mike Cosper and Yoram Hazony—their insights in their respective works on Esther will inspire and inform Max.
- Brett, Jenna, Rosie, Max, Andrea, Jeff, and Sara—a family tree with deep roots and abundant fruit.
- And Denalyn, the bride—each night Max will go to bed thinking, *I married an angel!* He will be right. She will be heaven-sent."

The two angels looked at the other and smiled, "With a team like this," one said, "even Lucado will be able to write."

Chapter One

SEARCHING FOR SPRINGTIME

Winter casts a cold shadow. The days are short. The nights are long. The sun seems shy, hidden behind the grayness. Warmth has packed her bags and migrated to the tropics. Beach weather would be nice.

But that's not going to happen. It's winter.

Spring will see blossoms. Summer sways leafy bushes in the wind. Autumn gives forth a harvest of plenty. But winter? Winter is still, deathly still. Fields are frosty. Trees extend skeletal limbs. Wildlife is silent. Gone.

Winter brings danger. Blizzards. Ice storms. Caution is the theme. Come springtime you'll run barefoot through the meadow and plunge into the pond. But now? It's best to button up, zip up, stay in, and stay safe.

It's winter out there.

Is it winter where you are? Are you trapped in a perpetual gloom? Do you know the solstice of sunless days and barren trees?

I know a mom who does. A mom of three kids. Two in diapers and one with a disability. Her apartment is small. Her income is meager. And her husband is AWOL. Life in Camp Chaos was too much for him. It's too much for her as well. But what choice does she have? Somebody always needs to be fed, changed, held, or bathed. So she does whatever needs doing, and it appears she will be doing it forever. She wonders if this winter will ever pass.

So does my friend Ed. He and I have much in common. Our health is good. Our golf game is poor. We both like dogs. We both have marriages that predate the Carter administration. The difference? My wife just asked me what I want for dinner. His keeps asking him who he is. He placed her in a memory-care facility a year ago. They'd dreamed of touring the country in an RV. So far he's spent his retirement sleeping alone and making daily visits to a woman who stares out the window.

Can you relate? When did you first realize that life was not going to turn out the way you thought?

Your parents divorced.

Your spouse cheated.

Your health never recovered.

Your friend never returned.

In that moment a Siberian cold settled over your life. Your world became an arctic circle of dark days, long nights, and bitter weather.

Winter.

This book was born in winter. As I pen these words, every person on the planet is living in the frostnip of COVID-19. A pandemic has locked us down. The mom I told you about? Her income is meager because her restaurant job was discontinued. Ed can still see his wife but only through a window. Church doors are closed. Students are stuck at home. Masks hide smiles. A microscopic virus has paralyzed us.

And an ancient sin threatens to undo us. Those of us who'd hoped racism was fading were convinced otherwise. An officer's knee on the neck of a Black man activated a subterranean anger. A volcano spewed into the streets of many cities.

The entire world seems wrapped in winter. We are all searching for springtime.

Winters are a part of life—some personal, some global—but all are powerful. Try as we might to bundle up and lean into the wind, the heartiest among us can fall. The wind is too strong. Nights are too long, and the question is all too common: Will this winter ever pass? You wonder (don't you wonder?) if you will survive this.

If so, God has a six-letter word of encouragement for you: E-S-T-H-E-R.

The book that bears her name was written to be read in wintertime. Written for the emotionally weary. Written for the person who feels outnumbered by foes, outmaneuvered by fate, and outdone by fear. It's as if God, in his kind providence, heard all the prayers of all the souls who have ever been stuck in an arctic February. To every person who has longed to see a green sprig on a barren branch, he says, "Follow me. I want you to see what I can do."

He escorts us to the front row of a grand theater and invites us to take a seat. He nods at the symphony conductor. The baton is lifted, the music begins, the curtain opens, and we are eyewitnesses to a triumph of divine drama.

The setting is the city of Susa in fifth century BC Persia (modern-day Iran). The empire was to its day what Rome was to the first century. During the reign of Darius I, also known as Darius the Great (522–486 BC), "it controlled more than 2.9 million square miles." The empire consisted of roughly 44 percent of the world's population, an estimated 50 million people.[1] It stretched some 4,464 miles from what is now Punjab, India, to Khartoum, Sudan.[2] To get the scope of it, walk from Los Angeles to Atlanta, turn around, and walk back to LA. Or, if you prefer, duplicate the United States map, set the two copies side by side, and you get a feel for the breadth of the Persian Empire.

The cast consists of a memorable quartet of characters.

Xerxes, the king, had a thirst for wine, a disregard for women, and convictions that changed with the weather. He ruled over Persia from 486 to 465 BC.[3] His name in Hebrew was Ahasuerus, which pronounced correctly sounds like a good sneeze. For that reason his name in Greek—Xerxes—will be my choice. (Besides, any name that makes double use of the letter *X* is fun to write.)

The book of Esther portrays him as a wimp, an accomplished drinker, but not much of a thinker. He was most comfortable holding a goblet and delegating decisions. The story attributes to him no profound thoughts or statesmanlike decrees. Catch him in the right mood, and he'd agree to genocide.

At least that was the experience of Haman, the villain in our story. His name sounds like "hangman," which is convenient, because this tyrant was all about death. He was a wealthy and influential officer in the cabinet of Xerxes. His jet was private. His wardrobe was tailored. He got manicures on Mondays and played golf with Xerxes on Thursdays. He had the ear of the king, the swagger of a pimp, and the compassion of Hitler.

Yes, that's accurate. We see a lot of Adolf in Haman. Both demanded to be worshipped. Both were intolerant of subversion. And both set out to exterminate the entire Jewish race. Can't you almost hear Hitler saying what Haman said?

> Then Haman said to King Ahasuerus, "There is a certain people scattered and dispersed among the people in all the provinces of your kingdom; their laws are different from all other people's, and they do not keep the king's laws. Therefore it is not fitting for the king to let them remain. If it pleases the king, let a decree be written that they be destroyed, and I will pay ten thousand talents of silver into the hands of those who do the work, to bring it into the king's treasuries." (Est. 3:8–9 NKJV)

Those "certain people" were none other than the Hebrew nation: the children of Israel, descendants of Abraham, and the family tree of Jesus Christ. They were scattered throughout the Persian Empire. To Haman they were inconsequential flecks of dandruff on the royal robe of Xerxes. But to God they were a chosen race through whom he would redeem humankind.

One of the exiled Jews really got under Haman's skin. His name was Mordecai. You're going to love him eventually. But you'll be puzzled by him initially. Quite content to be quiet, he chose to keep his ancestry under wraps. But a person could take only so much of Haman.

"Mordecai had a cousin . . . whom he had brought up" because she was an orphan. She must have been a head turner. Esther "had a lovely figure and was beautiful" (Est. 2:7). The ancient rabbinical writings position her as one of the four most beautiful women in the world, along with Sarah, Rahab, and Abigail.[4] She gained access to the king because of her appearance, but her story has relevance to yours because of her conviction and courage.

Are you sensing the elements of the drama?

A clueless brute of a king.

A devious, heartless, bloodthirsty Haman.

A nation of Jews under the threat of extermination.

Mordecai, defiant and determined.

Esther, gorgeous and gutsy.

And God? Where is God in the story? Aah, there's a question fit for the asking.

The book of Esther is known for being one of the two books in the Bible that never mention the name of God.[5] Until this point he has been everywhere, seemingly on every page. In Eden the Creator. In Ur the Prompter. In Egypt the Liberator. In the promised land the Warrior. But in Persia? The trail has grown cold.

At no point do we read "And God said" or "God chose" or "God decreed." There is no mention of the temple or the name *Yahweh* or *Elohim*, Hebrew nouns meaning God. There is no mention of apocalyptic visions, as Daniel saw, or concern for God's law, as Ezra expressed. Prayer is implied but not described. The seas do not split. The heavens do not roar. No dry bones come to life.

Why? Why the absence of spirituality? Why the seeming silence of God?

If you are in the midst of winter, you can relate to these questions. God may seem hidden to you. Distant. Removed. Absent from your script. Your world feels cut loose from the sun.

Others hear from God. You don't. Others say they know the will of God. You're bewildered. Others have a backstage pass to his performance. But you? You can't find his name on the playbill. Is he there? Does he care? You're unsure.

Might you be open to a gold nugget that lies in the substratum of the Esther story? Quiet providence. *Providence* is the two-dollar term theologians use to describe God's continuous control over history. He not only spoke the universe into being, but he governs it by his authority. He is "sustaining all things by his powerful word" (Heb. 1:3). He is regal, royal, and—this is essential—he is *right here*. He is not preoccupied with the plight of Pluto at the expense of your problems and pain.

He has been known to intervene dramatically. By his hand the Red Sea opened, the manna fell from heaven, a virgin gave birth, and a tomb gave life. Yet for every divine shout there are a million whispers. The book of Esther relates the story of our whispering God, who in unseen and inscrutable ways superintends all the actions and circumstances for the good of his people. This priceless book reminds us that he need not be loud to be strong. He need not cast a shadow to be present. God is still eloquent in his seeming silence and still active when he appears most distant.

> God is still eloquent in his seeming silence and still active when he appears most distant.

Does God seem absent to you?

If so, the book of Esther deserves your attention. Allow yourself to be caught up in the drama.

Act 1—*Confusion*: God's people choose the glamor of Persia over the goodness of God. Compromise replaces conviction. Confusion replaces clarity.

Act 2—*Crisis*: A decree of death places all Jews on life support. What hope does a fringe minority have in a pagan society?

Act 3—*Conquest*: The unimaginable happens. Something so unexpected that "sorrow turned to joy, [and their] mourning somersaulted into a holiday for parties and fun and laughter" (Est. 9:22 THE MESSAGE).

The theme of the book of Esther—indeed, the theme of the Bible—is that all the injustices of the world will be turned on their head. Grand reversals are God's trademark. When we feel as though everything is falling apart, God is working in our midst, causing everything to fall into place. He is the King of quiet providence, and he invites you and me to partner with him in his work. The headline of the book of Esther reads: *Relief will come. . . . Will you be a part of it?*

When all seems lost, it's not. When evil seems to own the day, God still has the final say. He has a Joseph for every famine and a David for every Goliath. When his people need rescuing, God calls a Rahab into service. When a baby Moses needs a mama, God prompts an Egyptian princess to have compassion. He always has his person.

> Grand reversals are God's trademark.

He had someone in the story of Esther.

And in your story he has you.

You want to retreat, stay quiet, stay safe, stay backstage. *I don't have what it takes*, you tell yourself. You could dismiss the "made for this moment" idea as mere folly.

But I oh-so-hope you won't.

Relief will come. . . . Will you be a part of it?

The headline of the

book of Esther reads:

Relief will come. . . .

Will you be a part of it?

This world gets messy, for sure. But God's solutions come through people of courage. People like Mordecai and Esther. People like you. People who dare to believe that they, by God's grace, were made to face a moment like this.

For those stuck in acts 1 and 2, be assured act 3 is on the way. In God's plan confusion and crisis give way to conquest. Winters don't last forever. Trees will soon bud. Snow will soon melt. Springtime is only a turn of the calendar away. For all we know God's hand is about to turn the page.

ACT 1
CONFUSION
FAITH IN A FAITHLESS WORLD

The couple sat wordlessly at the table. He picked at the lentil-and-lamb stew on his plate. She stared at the food on hers. "You've not taken a bite," he finally said. "You need to eat."

"I'm not hungry."

He began to object but then thought better of it. He looked at her young face, bathed in candlelight. Silken skin. High cheekbones. Brown eyes speckled with a hint of gold.

"Esther," he offered softly, "this is the best plan."

She raised her face to look at his. Moisture had gathered in her eyes, ready to spill. "But they will know. They will find out."

"Not if you are careful. Say little. Offer nothing. Go unnoticed."

Her eyes asked for help.

"Our people are adrift here in Susa. No one remembers Jerusalem. No one remembers the temple. Your parents—may their memory be blessed—lived and died in Persia. We will do the same. It's best to make the best of it."

"But he will demand so much of me."

Mordecai ran his fingers through his gray hair and then reached across the table for her hand. "We have no choice. The king has issued the order. The soldiers will come for you tomorrow. We cannot avoid the edict."

Mordecai sighed and stood and walked to the window. From his house in the citadel, he could faintly hear the evening prayers and see the flickering lights of Al-Yahudu, the town of the Judeans, a segregated community of Jews. He often looked out over the village but seldom visited it. Its residents didn't understand him. He, with his place in the court. He, with his buried identity. He, with his hidden faith.

And he didn't understand them. Can a person not manage more than one loyalty? A compromise here. A secret there. Fudge a few facts. Who's to know?

"Besides, Esther," he said as he turned to face her, "this could be our opportunity. Who knows what doors will open for us?"

"Yes, but who knows what we will lose in the process?" She stood and joined him at the window.

Mordecai placed an arm around her shoulders and whispered, "The Lord will be with you, as will I."

Chapter Two
DON'T GET COZY IN PERSIA

B lame it on the sudden warmth. Blame it on the welcome sight of buds on the trees. Blame it on a dash of young love.

But blame it mostly on a serious case of stupidity.

She and I were in college. We'd gone on a date or two and felt a spark or two. Spring was in the air. The gray sky had finally shed her cloudy coat. The Saturday afternoon sky was blue, and the breeze was warm. We drove through the countryside with windows down and spirits high. Was the ride planned or impromptu? I don't recall. What I do remember are the fields of winter wheat. So lush. So green. So inviting.

I'm sure the romp was my idea. I'm a bit prone to spontaneous folly. I once tried to impress a girl with a leaping plunge into a river, only to discover that it was three feet deep. Good thing I didn't dive. I sank up to my ankles in mud.

But back to the wheat field. Did I mention its beauty? An olive-green carpet, it was. Did I mention that romance was beginning to blossom? She for me. I for her. So when I suggested a barefoot scamper through the field, I was thinking hand in hand, skip and jump, and who knows—maybe a first kiss?

I stopped the car. We peeled off our shoes and socks and jumped over the fence, expecting to land on the equivalent of a soft mattress. But, alas, we'd been duped.

Winter wheat fields are green on the surface but rocky and sticky beneath. After three or four steps we came to a sudden stop. She gave me a what-were-you-thinking glare. By the time we retraced our steps, my ego was as bruised as our feet. That was the beginning of the end for us. The day love died in a West Texas wheat field. (Sounds like a country song.)

You've made the same mistake. Not on a farm, but in life. You have been fooled. Deceived. Tricked. Lured into a field of green only to realize it was a bed of thorns.

Remember how the bright lights led to lonely nights? How the promise of fast cash led to dead-end debt? Remember the time he lured you into his bed or she convinced you of her love? You didn't bloody your feet, but you broke your heart or drained your bank account and, I hope, learned this lesson: things aren't always what they seem. What's too good to be true usually is.

> Tough times can trigger poor decisions.

This is a word to the wise. And this is a relevant warning for those who are stuck in winter. Tough times can trigger poor decisions. We lose our bearings. We forget God's call. We exchange our convictions for the bright lights of Persia. This was the temptation that faced the Jews.

Here is the way the story begins:

> In the third year of his reign [Xerxes] gave a banquet for all his nobles and officials. The military leaders of Persia and Media, the princes, and the nobles of the provinces were present. (Est. 1:3)

Xerxes' excuse for this lavish event was to convince Persian nobles, officials, princes, governors, and military leaders to support his campaign against the Greeks.[1] The citadel, his seat of power, towered over the city. It was visible for miles. Its immensity sent a message: in these halls walks an important king. "Hear ye him!"

Xerxes was thirty-five years of age and rich beyond imagination. His palace boasted "hangings of white and blue linen . . . couches of gold and silver on a mosaic pavement of porphyry, marble, mother-of-pearl and other costly stones" (v. 6). The palace hall had thirty-six columns that stood seventy feet tall. Each column was crowned with sculptures of twin bulls, which supported the immense wooden timbers of the ceiling.[2] Even the mosaic pavements were works of art. When Alexander the Great entered the palace at Susa a century later, he discovered, in today's dollars, the equivalent of $54.5 billion in bullion and 270 tons of minted gold coins.[3] Xerxes was not hurting for cash.

He promised wealth and rewards to all willing warriors. And to prove he could make good on his promise, he staged a six-month Vegas extravaganza. "For a full 180 days he displayed the vast wealth of his kingdom and the splendor and glory of his majesty. When these days were over, the king gave a banquet, lasting seven days, in the enclosed garden of the king's palace, for all the people from the least to the greatest who were in the citadel of Susa" (vv. 4–5).

It was a Mardi Gras of drinking and dining. Guests from a hundred posts and ports. Officials, power brokers, and wannabes mingled, schmoozed, and indulged. Feasts on a dozen tables. Wine was water. Everyone imbibed as much as they desired, then drank some more. Six months of fine food, who's who, pinot noir, and excess. Xerxes presided over the whole event.

But toward the end of the carnival, the king's true colors began to appear. On his 187th day of feasting, when he was "in high spirits from wine" (v. 10), he sent for Queen Vashti. A bit tipsy, Xerxes decided to show off his wife. She "was lovely to look at" (v. 11). Apparently he expected her to dance in front of his frat friends and leave them entranced in a cloud of perfume.

According to the Midrash, an ancient commentary on Esther, Xerxes told his queen to enter the room wearing nothing but a crown.[4] That detail cannot be verified. But this much is sure: he did not invite

Vashti in order to hear her opinions on matters of state. He wanted to flaunt her in front of his poker pals.

Persia was not a safe place for a woman. Females, including the queen, were property. Vashti spent most of her time cloistered in some corner, pampered and preened for her next appearance before the king. She was an accoutrement, nothing more, a trophy in his case. Her only function was to make Xerxes look potent and important.

Boy, was he in for a surprise. She refused to comply. Prance about in front of a bunch of bibulous males? No thank you. (Good for you, Vashti.)

"The king became furious and burned with anger" (v. 12).

A chuckle is permitted here. Big, strong, billionaire Xerxes, ruler of 127 provinces,[5] mighty overlord who controlled the world, was undone by his wife. He'd spent six months wining, dining, and flexing his muscles. Yet on the last night he was made to look namby-pamby in front of his drinking buddies. When the ruler showed off, his incompetency showed up. He was so taken aback that he called a committee meeting. He assembled his seven (barely sober) advisors and said, "Duh, . . . what am I supposed to do?"

Wiser consultants would have urged the king to settle the matter in private. They would have reminded the king that six months of wine can fog the mind and would have suggested that he let his brain clear a bit. But Xerxes was blessed with cabinet members who were seemingly as dense and drunk as he. They huddled, strategized, and gave this bizarre report.

Queen Vashti has done wrong, not only against the king but also against all the nobles and the peoples of all the provinces of King Xerxes. For the queen's conduct will become known to all the women, and so they will despise their husbands and say, "King Xerxes commanded Queen Vashti to be brought before him, but she would not come." (vv. 16–17)

I smell fear in those words. "Fellows, we've got to act. Something has to be done. If not, the world might spin off its axis."

Women will begin thinking for themselves.

Men will need to be kind to their wives.

Daughters will envision a life outside the kitchen!

How to avoid such a tragedy? Banish Vashti.

Let it be written in the laws of Persia and Media, which cannot be repealed, that Vashti is never again to enter the presence of King Xerxes. Also let the king give her royal position to someone else who is better than she. Then when the king's edict is proclaimed throughout all his vast realm, all the women will respect their husbands, from the least to the greatest. (vv. 19–20)

On what planet were these men born? Who spiked their wine with silly juice? Were they really so blind, so arrogant, so out of touch with human nature that they thought an edict would engender the devotion of a gender? And these men oversaw the running of the largest empire in the world? A bunch of locker-room punks is what they were.

Xerxes' display of importance (party, possessions, power) became Xerxes' display of ignorance (temper, indecisiveness, folly). For all his strut and swagger, Xerxes was nothing more than a misogynistic chump.

Do you see the irony? Do you shake your head at the folly? Does the response of Xerxes cause you to roll your eyes in disgust? If so, the mission of the author is accomplished. The story of the insolent Xerxes and the story of my romp in a winter-wheat field posit the same possibility. What if the glitz and glamour are only folly and foibles? What if the lure of lights is a hoax? All the red carpets. All the social media pictures. All the fancy parties and invitation-only clubs. What if all the whoop-de-do and la-di-da are one big field of winter wheat?

Don't romp in it.

Don't fall for it.

Don't buy the line.

Don't take the bait.

Don't take the bluff.

Don't get cozy in Persia.

Stay faithful to your call as a covenant people.

Let's widen our lens for a bit of context. Do you have time for a few paragraphs of Hebrew history?

When God called Abraham out of Ur, he made a covenant—a promise—that Abraham would be the father of a holy nation. "I will bless those who bless you, and I will place a curse on those who harm you. And all the people on earth will be blessed through you" (Gen. 12:3 NCV).

Exactly how would God bless the world through Israel? First, they would model a way of living that reflected the glory and goodness of God. Unlike the depraved, promiscuous, violent Canaanites who surrounded them, they would worship their Maker, love their neighbors, and honor their families. Second, they would provide a lineage through whom Jesus Christ, the greatest global blessing, could be born. The children of Israel were the curators and caretakers of God's covenant to Abraham.

For this reason they were to remain separate. Different. Holy. Set apart. They were not permitted to marry non-Jews, worship pagan deities, or embrace the pagan culture. They had distinct ways to worship, live, and love.

Did they succeed at being separate? Sometimes marvelously so. (Think Joshua inheriting the promised land.) Sometimes, miserably, no. (Think the long line of corrupt kings, each more wicked than the prior one.) Eventually the people so forgot their God that he used exile to get their attention.

In 586 BC the Babylonians sacked Jerusalem and deported about ten thousand of the city's elite. In 539 BC the Persians sacked the

Babylonians. By the time we meet Mordecai and Esther, the Jews were three generations and more than a thousand miles removed from their days in Jerusalem.

It's hard to imagine that any of them recalled life in their homeland. They were encircled by Persians. They daily heard the footsteps of the soldiers and the wheels of the chariots. Merchants did business with non-Jews. Farmers sold their produce to Persians. They lived amid the opulent wealth and fragrant temples of foreign people. What's more, the truly zealous Jews had taken the opportunity to return to Jerusalem either with Zerubbabel[6] or with Ezra.[7]

The Jews who remained in Persia *chose* to remain in Persia. Exile had been kind to them. They had good jobs, secure positions. Some were more Persian than they were Hebrew. To enjoy the success and wealth of the people in Susa, all they had to do was play their cards right, abide by the rules, and fade into the fabric of the culture.

Unlike other books of the Old Testament that describe the Jews settling and settled in the promised land, the book of Esther depicts a people who are distant from their land. Jerusalem was so far away, and Persia was, well, so relevant, so lush, so inviting. It was a gigantic wheat field. The author didn't use my metaphor but would have appreciated it. The point of the first chapter of Esther is simply this: Persia is lying to you.

Do we need the same reminder? The assignment given to the Jews has been passed on to us. God displays his glory and goodness through the church. As we worship God, love our neighbors, and cherish our families, we become billboards of God's message.

We, too, are caretakers. Caretakers of the message of Jesus. He was born through the lineage of the Jews. Today he is born through the lives of his saints. As you and I live out our faith, he is delivered into a faith-famished culture. We have the hope this world needs.

But sometimes we forget our calling. We need this reminder. Persia is lying to us. I don't mean to be blunt, but, then again, I do.

As we worship God, love
our neighbors, and cherish
our families, we become
billboards of God's message.

Billion-dollar industries are conning you by luring you into lifestyles that will leave you wounded and weary.

Examples? Try this one. *Pornography is a harmless expression of sexuality.* Really? It is as addictive as drugs and alcohol.[8] It changes the makeup of the brain.[9] What about the sex trafficking it encourages, the violence it engenders? Yet the message that porn peddlers whisper to the unsuspecting is "It won't hurt. It's just sex."

Liar.

Or this: *Whoever dies with the most toys wins.* You are what you own, so own all you can. Take on the liability. Borrow the money. Saddle yourself with a budget-busting mortgage; it is worth it. The average American household carries more than $145,000 in debt, including nearly $7,000 in credit card debt.[10] We worship stuff, hoping stuff will bring life. But your Maker? He tells you the truth: "Do not lay up for yourselves treasures on earth, where moth and rust destroy . . . but lay up for yourselves treasures in heaven" (Matt. 6:19–20 NKJV).

Here is one more falsehood. *A few drinks take the edge off the day. What could be wrong?* According to the marketing machine behind the liquor industry, the answer would be "Nothing at all."

"Enjoy the high life," says Miller beer.

"Find your beach," beckons Corona Extra.

"The happiest hour on earth," boasts Jameson Whiskey.

"A shot of adventure," claims Jose Cuervo tequila.[11]

Yet underneath the slick advertisements lies an ugly underbelly of alcohol abuse. Excessive drinking takes its toll on bodies, mental health, marriages, work, friendships, productivity, and pregnancies.[12]

The list of lies could go on for chapters. Deceptions about identity, race, pluralism. They are everywhere. And their consequences are devastating.

At the time of this writing, depression is on the rise,[13] divorce filings are up 34 percent year to year,[14] calls to mental health hotlines have increased 891 percent,[15] and the suicide rate is the highest it has been at any time since World War II.[16] One in four people ages eighteen through twenty-four seriously considered suicide in the thirty days prior to being surveyed.[17]

How do God's people live in a godless society? Blend in and assimilate? No, this is the time to stand out and assist. We were made for this moment.

During my Boy Scout days I earned a first-aid merit badge. I could be counted on to wrap a sprained ankle or bandage a scraped knee. During one of our daylong jamborees, I was assigned a spot in the first-aid tent. Initially I was thrilled. I wore a first-aid armband and stood under a first-aid flag. I felt important. But as I stood outside and watched the activities, I began to feel left out. The other scouts were running, swimming, competing, and playing. And Max? I was standing at the front of the tent. I wanted to remove my armband and join the fun. A scoutmaster heard my complaint and reminded me, "You have a special place here. You need to be different. This tent is the place for hurting kids."

So I kept my post.

Will you keep yours?

This is no time to play around in Persia.

> This is the time to stand out and assist. We were made for this moment.

You are a chosen people, a royal priesthood, a holy nation, God's special possession, that you may declare the praises of him who called you out of darkness into his wonderful light. Once you were not a people, but now you are the people of God; once you had not received mercy, but now you have received mercy.

Dear friends, I urge you, as foreigners and exiles, to abstain from sinful desires, which wage war against your soul. Live such

You were made for more
than moody kings and flashy
parties. You were made to
serve the almighty God and
be a temple of his Holy Spirit.

good lives among the pagans that, though they accuse you of doing wrong, they may see your good deeds and glorify God on the day he visits us. (1 Peter 2:9–12)

You were made for more than moody kings and flashy parties. You were made to serve the almighty God and be a temple of his Holy Spirit. Persia offers nothing. Hollywood can't satisfy your needs. Madison Avenue makes big promises but leaves people naked of hope. Godless living is no life to live.

Will Mordecai and Esther see this? Cast in a story of decadence, will they resist the allure? Which will triumph—faith or façade? The answer might surprise you. The answer might *caution* you. Heroes of the Bible don't always begin that way. Like you and me, they've been known to romp on the wrong side of the fence.

I don't want to give away the details of the next chapter, but suffice it to say, our main characters are soon to have sore feet.

Chapter Three

THE GIRL WITH TWO NAMES

I have two questions to bring up in heaven. Not complaints, because we will have no complaints. And I'm not sure we will have questions. If we do, I'd like clarity on two topics: mosquitos and middle school. Was either one necessary? Wouldn't the world have been better off without those little blood-sucking varmints and those in-between, off-balance years of middle school?

I was a nerd as an adolescent. Horribly shy. Had you asked me to choose between a chat with a girl and a root canal, I would have gone to the dentist. I had two bookworm buddies. We weren't cool. We didn't dress classy or talk the lingo. We studied. We actually had competitions to see who made the best grades. We sat in the front row of each class. We wore—hang on to your slide rule—pocket protectors! We were nerds. Which was fine with me until one geek moved away and the other got a paper route, and as quick as you can say "solitary," I was. Bepimpled, gangly, and socially awkward.

I had one thing going for me: I could play baseball. Not great, but good enough for my father to convince me to try out for Pony League and good enough to get selected. Pony League, in case you don't know, bridges those unwieldy years between Little League and high school. I was a newcomer on a squad of seventh and eighth graders.

The first day of practice was a cold day in March. The winter wind kept spring at bay. A blue norther dropped the mercury and bent the barely budding trees. Mom gave me a sweatshirt to wear. It bore the emblem of Abilene Christian College, a fine liberal arts institution from which my sisters had graduated and where I would eventually do the same. I was already in the car en route to the practice—my first practice with studly upperclassmen—when I pulled on the sweatshirt and saw the words "Abilene Christian." I was mortified. I could not show up wearing a shirt that bore the name "Christian." Cool kids aren't Christians. The in crowd isn't Christian. I couldn't debut as a Christian. The odds were already stacked against me. I was a Poindexter and a rookie.

The confession of what I did next might result in my defrocking. When Mom dropped me off at the practice field, I waited until she was out of view, and then I peeled off the shirt. I wadded it into a ball and stuck it in the base of the backstop. Rather than risk being left out by the team, I chose to shiver in short sleeves.

No, I'm not proud of my choice. The apostle Paul was speaking to the middle school version of Max when he wrote: "Do not conform to the pattern of this world, but be transformed by the renewing of your mind" (Rom. 12:2).

We can conform or be transformed. On that day I chose to wad up the shirt.

Esther and Mordecai did the same. They disguised their identity. They conformed.

Does it trouble you to hear me say that? We tend to see Esther and Mordecai as rock solid. She, the female version of Daniel. He, a steel-spined Paul Revere. They never wavered, never floundered, never shirked their duty. They saved the Jewish nation, for crying out loud. Carve their faces on the Hebrew Mount Rushmore. They took a courageous stand.

> We can conform or be transformed.

But not before they didn't.

Bible characters are complex. They aren't one-dimensional felt figures that fit easily into a

Sunday school curriculum box. Moses was a murderer before he was a liberator. Joseph was a punk before he was a prince. Yes, the apostle Peter proclaimed Christ on the day of Pentecost. But he also denied Christ on the eve of the crucifixion. The people of the Bible were exactly that: people. Real people. Like you. Like me. And, like you and me, they had their good moments, and, well, they were known to hide their faith.

Chapter 2 of Esther opens with the phrase "after these things."

> After these things, when the wrath of King Ahasuerus subsided, he remembered Vashti, what she had done, and what had been decreed against her. (v. 1 NKJV)

"After these things." After what things? What events had transpired between chapters 1 and 2? A clue to the answer is found later in the text. "Esther was taken to King Xerxes at the royal palace in early winter of the seventh year of his reign" (v. 16 NLT).

Our story began in the "third year of his reign" (1:3). Four years have passed since Vashti's humiliation of Xerxes. During these four years Xerxes made an ambitious but disastrous attempt to invade Greece. It's safe to imagine him weary and dispirited. Upon his return "he remembered Vashti." He realized that he had no queen. He entered the gilded gate to no outstretched arms. No wife gave him comfort or offered him encouragement. Perhaps it was a wounded ego that prompted him to take the advice of his counselors and replace Vashti with "someone else who is better than she" (v. 19), code language for someone who will show up, shut up, and make the king look good.

The order went out to conscript the most beautiful virgins from the vast empire so Xerxes could make his choice. Estimates as to the number of candidates range from 400 to 1,460.[1] Bible class retellings of this decree fail to describe its atrocities. The girls were not asked to love him, just entertain him. The inexperienced and no doubt terrified candidates abandoned their own aspirations and dreams for the whims of an insecure monarch. Fail to be selected and the young woman would spend the rest of her life as one of his concubines. She could not return to her family. She would see the king only at his request. The children she conceived with him would be raised to serve the court but would not be considered heirs to the throne.[2] She would never sleep with another man so that the king need never risk that another man, in the dark of night, be told that he was a better lover than Xerxes.[3]

Sickening, I know.

Into this toxic stew called Persia fell a Jew named Mordecai and his cousin Hadassah.

> Now there was in the citadel of Susa a Jew of the tribe of Benjamin, named Mordecai son of Jair, the son of Shimei, the son of Kish, who had been carried into exile from Jerusalem by Nebuchadnezzar king of Babylon, among those taken captive with Jehoiachin king of Judah. (2:5–6)

You and I read that paragraph with no reaction. We might comment on the hard-to-pronounce names, but that's it. But to the postexilic Jews? Trained in the ways of the Torah? Taught to cherish their identity as God's covenant people? That paragraph would arch a few eyebrows and raise a few questions.

For example, why was Mordecai in the citadel of Susa? To live in the citadel was to live on the equivalent of Capitol Hill. The fortress was the epicenter of Persian influence and government. Most Jews, exiled as they were, lived away from the citadel, far removed from the heart of Persian power and politics. Mordecai not only lived in the citadel, but he was also "on duty at the palace" (v. 21 TLB).

He worked for Xerxes! Mordecai placed himself in the thick of the political thicket. Again, you and I are twenty-five hundred years and thousands of pages of history removed. No big deal. Good for you, Mordecai. You've made the big time in a foreign land. But to the Jews? That was a big deal. Remember, to be a Jew was to be called out and set apart. But Mordecai was on the payroll of a pagan king.

What's more, he had a pagan name! "Mordecai" was an adaptation of "Marduk," a Persian male deity.[4] Mordecai's theonym memorialized a foreign god. Would a modern-day Jew name his son Muhammad? Would a God-fearing Jew in our day work for the Iranian military? Not likely. Then how do we explain a Jew named after a pagan numen and living on the Persian payroll?

An answer might be found by returning to the hard-to-pronounce words. Mordecai was the "son of Jair, the son of Shimei, the son of Kish, who had been carried into exile from Jerusalem by Nebuchadnezzar king of Babylon, among those taken captive with Jehoiachin king of Judah" (vv. 5–6). Mordecai was three generations removed from Jerusalem, plenty of time for the lines of Hebrew distinctiveness to fade. Living out the pagan name he was given, Mordecai went clandestine with his convictions. He had wadded up the sweatshirt and stuffed it at the base of the backstop.

He instructed Esther to follow suit.

> Mordecai had a cousin named Hadassah, whom he had brought up because she had neither father nor mother. This young woman, who was also known as Esther, had a lovely figure and was beautiful. Mordecai had taken her as his own daughter when her father and mother died. (v. 7)

Hadassah comes from the Hebrew word for *myrtle*. According to some rabbinical commentaries, *myrtle* implies "righteous."[5] The name fits. Hadassah will soon take a righteous stand.

But she was also called Esther in deference to the Persian goddess Ishtar.[6] How did she get this name? And how do we explain the decision of Mordecai to enter Esther in the contest to be queen of Persia?

When we first met Xerxes, you'll recall that he gave Vashti the boot because she refused to behave like a sugar baby. Next he solicited all the young beauties of Persia to apply for the now-vacant position.

> When the king's order and edict had been proclaimed, many young women were brought to the citadel of Susa and put under the care of Hegai. Esther also was taken to the king's palace and entrusted to Hegai, who had charge of the harem. She pleased him and won his favor. . . .
>
> Esther had not revealed her nationality and family background, because Mordecai had forbidden her to do so. (vv. 8–10)

Let's tally this up. Mordecai hid his heritage and taught his young cousin to do the same. He entered her in a bachelorette contest, knowing that the competition included a night in the bed of a Gentile king. He told her to show him a good time and keep her nationality a secret. She complied.

What in the world is going on here?

Like the Babylonians before them, polytheistic Persians did not require their conquered peoples to give up their gods. Go ahead, they said. Sacrifice to your cow, pray to your moon, bow before your goddess; just worship the gods of Persia too.

This proved problematic for the Jews. According to their Torah there was only one God. Every Jew worth his matzo bread quoted the Shema twice daily: "Listen, people of Israel! The LORD our God is the only LORD. Love the LORD your God with all your heart, all your soul, and all your strength" (Deut. 6:4–5 NCV). They were to worship Jehovah God only and have no other god before him. So how were they to behave in Persia? The question of the psalmist is the question of the book of Esther. "How shall we sing the LORD's song in a foreign land?" (Ps. 137:4 NKJV). How does a person of faith live in a faithless world?

The initial response of Mordecai and Esther was disguise and compromise. The soft butter of their convictions melted against the warm knife of pragmatism.

Why risk angering the king?

What good comes from disclosure of the truth?

I can worship the Persian gods and God, right?

I can change my name and work for the king, right?

I can keep my identity a secret and sleep with the king, right?

They created a world of hidden identity. Mordecai kept his Hebrew ancestry a secret. Esther maneuvered through the queen-search contest without disclosing that she was a daughter of Abraham. By the time we meet Mordecai and Esther, they've buried their Jewish identity beneath several layers of compromise.

Which brings to mind another question for me to ask in heaven. In addition to clarification about mosquitos and middle school, I'd like a moment with Mr. Mordecai. "Why did you do it?" I'd inquire. "Why let them take her? You knew what would happen. She would be spruced up for one night and then lose her virginity to a brute. Unless selected as queen, she'd spend the rest of her life as a cloistered concubine. How many laws of the Torah did you violate?"

I'm thinking Mordecai would respond in one of two ways.

- "Max, you weren't there. You don't know how crazy Xerxes was. He was a fickle, psychotic dictator. In this way my precious Esther would at least be safe. That's why I told her to tell no one that she was a Jew. I wanted to protect her."

Or . . .

- "Max you don't get it. This was all a part of my plan. I worked in the palace. I made friends with Hegai, head of the harem. I told him about her and her about him. We set the whole thing in motion. But if he knew her nationality . . ."

Then again . . .

- Mordecai might very well say, "Lucado, who are you to question me? You're the one who was too embarrassed to wear the sweatshirt."

He would be right to push back. The compulsion to hide our identity as children of God affects us all. Not in Persia but at work, school, on the bowling league, and in the Pony League. But at some point each of us has to figure out who we are and what that identity means for our lives.

> The compulsion to hide our identity as children of God affects us all.

We face the identical temptation that Mordecai and Esther faced. Our society permits all beliefs except an exclusive one. Do whatever you want as long as you applaud what everyone else does. The incontestable value of Western culture is tolerance. Ironically, the champions of tolerance are intolerant of a religion like Christianity that adheres to one Savior and one solution to the human problem. To believe in Jesus as the only Redeemer is to incur the disdain of Persia.

Are we not tempted to peel off the sweatshirt? In such moments God's message is clear: remember your name. "What marvelous love the Father has extended to us! Just look at it—we're called children of God! That's who we really are" (1 John 3:1 THE MESSAGE).

Every parent who has sent a child to camp, class, or college knows the dry-mouthed fear of the farewell moment. There is a frantic

You are the presence of

Jesus in this world—an

eternal being, destined

for an eternal home. You

are a citizen of heaven.

scramble for words. What advice can I give? What parting wisdom? Though the words take many forms, most are a version of this: "I love you. Don't forget that. And don't forget who you are. You are mine!"

Do you know who you are? And whose you are?

You are the presence of Jesus in this world—an eternal being, destined for an eternal home. Pimply faced and gangly? Hogwash. You are a citizen of heaven. Unique in all of creation. Secured by Christ for eternity. The devil can't touch you. The demons can't have you. The world can't possess you. What people think about you matters not one whit. You belong to your heavenly Father.

I received an unexpected reminder about my identity a few weeks ago. My wife and I had the opportunity to drive through my hometown and pay respects at the grave site of my mom and dad. It'd been ten years since our last visit. It is easy to locate their burial spot. It is the only one with a live oak tree. The cemetery has many trees, mind you, but only one live oak. I can't explain my dad's fondness for this Texas tree. They have gnarly, knuckled trunks and tend to grow in all angles. But for some reason Dad took such a liking to them that he planted one over his burial plot. He'd just been diagnosed with ALS, and wanting to get his affairs in order, he requested permission to plant the tree.

He took me to see it. Barely a sapling it was. So small that I could wrap my hand around it and touch finger to thumb. That was three and a half decades ago. Today the trunk is as thick as a man's torso, and its branches extend far over the grave site. But it wasn't the size of the tree that impressed me; it was what my dad had carved.

A heart. I'd never noticed it. He etched the design and scraped out the bark so that as the tree has grown, so has the carving. In the center of the heart are the initials of his kids. When the tree was small, the heart was small as well. But as the tree has expanded, so has the message. He never told us that he did this. I suppose he wanted to leave a surprise. He knew we would need a reminder of his love, so he left it notched into the trunk. *You have a place in my heart.*

Your Father did the same. Not with a live oak tree, but with a cross. Not with a carving, but with the crimson blood of Christ. Years have passed, and the heart of the cross, the message of the cross, has only grown.

To the middle school version of Max, God says, "Look at Jesus Christ on the tree of Calvary. Let me tell you who you are. You are made special by the work of Christ."

Like me, you've had, and will have, your sweatshirt moments. In those moments remember who you are.

Moreover, remember that the story of Mordecai and Esther didn't stop at chapter 2. You are only a page from a fifth century BC version of a come-to-Jesus moment. Our duo will recall their identity, reach for their discarded sweatshirts, and put them back on. They will accept God's invitation to partner with him, and God, who is so happy to give his children a second chance, will put them straight to work.

I wish I could report that I did the same. But I didn't. I nearly froze that day as I stood short sleeved in left field. Sometimes we are left searching for springtime, not because of God's choice, but because of our foolish ones.

Is it time for you to come in out of the cold?

ACT 2
CRISIS

COURAGE IN A HOSTILE LAND

Mordecai's morning began with no agenda. He washed his face and had his breakfast of figs and pomegranates. He selected a robe from an assortment he had gathered over the years and left his house for the brief walk to the city gates.

The sun was warm. The merchants were busy. Dogs barked. Children played. He patted the rump of a donkey. He grabbed a handful of nuts from the basket of a vendor and tossed him a coin. He greeted associates and acknowledged the arrival of dignitaries. They came every day. All wanted an audience with Xerxes to gain his blessing, money, favor, alliance. Mordecai and others made sure they were welcomed and vetted.

As Mordecai neared the archway, he heard his name. "Mordecai!"

He turned to see Hegai, the head of the harem.

"You're out early, old friend," Mordecai replied. "Is someone giving away free food?"

He expected a smile. None appeared. Just a breathless report.

"He's coming out any minute. You don't want to be near when he passes."

Mordecai looked at Hegai and nodded. Haman was to be avoided at all costs. Ever since the king had named him vice regent, the citadel had been on edge. Haman snarled at all he saw. He barked orders and demanded obedience. The king required that everyone bow in Haman's presence, but Mordecai and Hegai knew that the order was not the king's idea.

The two men scurried to the shadows. Thus far they had managed to avoid the thug and his entourage. But not this time.

"Prepare the way for the king's man!" shouted a soldier. "All must stop and pay homage!"

Hegai cursed under his breath. "We're getting too old. Next time we will run faster."

He lowered himself to the ground and turned to whisper to his friend, but Mordecai had not knelt. Hegai cut his eyes toward the gate. The large doors were open. The horses and the riders were in sight. Haman was only seconds from appearing. And Mordecai? He was still standing.

"Mordecai!" Hegai whispered. "Down!"

Mordecai ignored him. His eyes filled with anger and resolve. The sight of Haman had triggered a suppressed rage.

"You!" demanded a soldier. "Kneel before the king's man!"

Mordecai stared. Haman stopped. And the eyes of the two men met.

Chapter Four

HE REFUSED
TO BOW

In February 2015 the terrorist group ISIS beheaded twenty-one Christians on a beach in Libya. In a video the men are seen moments before their execution, calling out to Jesus and mouthing prayers. Most of them were Egyptian migrant laborers working to provide for their families.

ISIS slaughtered the men in order to shock the world with terror. The response of their families sent an altogether different message. One mother of a twenty-five-year-old victim said, "I'm proud of my son. He did not change his faith till the last moment of death. I thank God. . . . He is taking care of him."[1]

A priest described his congregation, which lost thirteen of its men, by saying, "The whole congregation was coming to the church to pray for their return, but in their prayers later on, they asked that if they died, they die for their faith, and that's what happened. The congregation is actually growing, psychologically and spiritually."[2]

The men could have lived. With a simple confession of Allah, knives would have been lowered and lives spared.

What would you have done?

The question is more than academic. You may not face blades and terrorists, but don't you face critics and accusers? Family members mock your beliefs. Professors make fun of your faith. Colleagues gossip about your convictions. Do you sometimes feel all alone?

Mordecai did.

As many as five years have passed since Esther was appointed queen (Est. 2:16–17 and 3:7). Life has been good to her and Mordecai. She lives in the lap of luxury. He serves in a seat of power. Both continue to keep their Jewish nationality a secret. As far as anyone knows, they are pure Persian. All is good until Mordecai overhears a plot.

> In those days, while Mordecai sat within the king's gate, two of the king's eunuchs, Bigthan and Teresh, doorkeepers, became furious and sought to lay hands on King Ahasuerus. So the matter became known to Mordecai, who told Queen Esther, and Esther informed the king in Mordecai's name. And when an inquiry was made into the matter, it was confirmed, and both were hanged on a gallows; and it was written in the book of the chronicles in the presence of the king. (2:21–23 NKJV)

The Persian versions of John Wilkes Booth and Lee Harvey Oswald schemed to assassinate King Xerxes, but their big mouths got them into trouble. Mordecai caught wind of the plot, reported them to Esther, and they ended up on the king's gallows.

And . . . that's it. No more details. No public recognition for Mordecai. No more character development. No explanation. My editors would red ink me. "Why include this story?" "Who are these people?" "What happened next?"

A possible answer is found in the first verse of the next chapter. "After these events, King Xerxes honored Haman son of Hammedatha, the Agagite, elevating him and giving him a seat of honor higher than that of all the other nobles" (3:1).

Xerxes found himself exposed again. His first wife had resisted him, and now his subjects were plotting to kill him. He presumed to be lord over the world's greatest empire and yet was threatened from within his own camp. A statement must be made! He responded by appointing a heavy-handed, take-no-prisoners vizier, "Haman son of Hammedatha, the Agagite."

Don't hurry past the odd-sounding terms in this introduction. Haman was the son of *Hammedatha, the Agagite*. An Agagite was a descendent of Agag, the king of the Amalekites. The Amalekites were the most ancient of the Hebrews' enemies. The children of Israel were hardly out of Egyptian bondage when "Amalek came and fought with Israel in Rephidim" (Ex. 17:8 NKJV).

Why would a warring tribe turn their wrath against some ex-slaves? Moses and his people owned no land. They possessed no territory. They had done nothing to anger the Amalekites. Why the guerrilla warfare on the Hebrew people?

And why with such cruelty? Moses recalled their barbarism when he urged the Israelites to "remember what the Amalekites did to you along the way when you came out of Egypt. When you were weary and worn out, they met you on your journey and attacked all who were lagging behind; they had no fear of God. . . . [Y]ou shall blot out the name of Amalek from under heaven. Do not forget!" (Deut. 25:17–19).

The Amalekites picked off the stragglers: the old, the sick, the widowed, the disabled. They had not the courage to attack from the front. Moses saw the evil people for who they were: instruments of Satan. Lucifer hated the Jews. He knew God's plan was to redeem the world through Jesus, and he made it his aim to annihilate the family tree before it could bear fruit. After defeating the Amalekites in the wilderness, God promised, "'I will utterly blot out the remembrance of Amalek from under heaven.' And Moses . . . said, 'Because the LORD has sworn: the LORD will have war with Amalek from generation to generation'" (Ex. 17:14–16 NKJV).

God went so far as to command King Saul to destroy all the Amalekites, along with all their animals. But Saul spared the king and saved the best of the sheep. The name of the king? Agag. Haman, then, was a descendant of the original anti-Semitic race. Hebrew hatred was in his blood.

Mordecai, in turn, was a descendant of Saul, a Benjamite (Est. 2:5). Saul's refusal to obey God and destroy Agag was a perpetual blemish on the Benjamite legacy.

The moment Mordecai encountered Haman in Susa was more than two men meeting at the citadel. This was a collision of ten centuries of bias and hatred.

Haman and his hate made for high drama when he saw Mordecai at the gate. "All the royal officials at the king's gate knelt down and paid honor to Haman, for the king had commanded this concerning him. But Mordecai would not kneel down or pay him honor" (3:2).

Someone needs to capture this moment on canvas. The towering gate in the background. Haughty Haman and his entourage of servants. Persian officials with faces low to the ground. And in their midst one man standing ramrod straight—Mordecai. Backbone as stiff as a frigate mast.

This was the moment Mordecai refused to bow.

His resistance went on day after day. His fellow court members "spoke to him daily and he would not listen to them." Finally they got an explanation. "Mordecai had told them that he was a Jew" (v. 4 NKJV).

Well, there it is. The camouflage came off. The mask was removed. Mordecai had spent his life hiding his nationality and had trained Esther to do the same. The two were so Persian in tone, appearance, language, and behavior that she could marry the king, he could work for the king, and no one knew that they were descendants of Abraham. But one look at Haman changed that. Mordecai wasn't about to bow before an enemy of God's people.

Haman went ballistic. Place Esther 3:5–6 against your nose, take a whiff, and see if you don't detect the stench of Satan:

When Haman saw that Mordecai would not kneel down or pay him honor, he was enraged. Yet having learned who Mordecai's people were, he scorned the idea of killing only Mordecai. Instead Haman looked for a way to destroy all Mordecai's people, the Jews, throughout the whole kingdom of Xerxes.

It wasn't enough to make Mordecai miserable. It wasn't enough to kill the unbending Jew. Haman embarked on a mission to annihilate God's chosen people, root and branch.

This was bald-faced racism. Haman felt superior to an entire race of human beings simply because of their ancestry. As if he had the right to gamble with the lives of humans, Haman took the equivalent of a die called *pur*, cast the lot, and determined the date of execution to be eleven months hence. He then went to the potentate and said:

> There is a certain people dispersed among the peoples in all the provinces of your kingdom who keep themselves separate. Their customs are different from those of all other people, and they do not obey the king's laws; it is not in the king's best interest to tolerate them. If it pleases the king, let a decree be issued to destroy them, and I will give ten thousand talents of silver to the king's administrators for the royal treasury. (vv. 8–9)

Haman was willing to pay $20 million[3] for the right to exterminate the Jews.[4] By now we know that Haman was vile to the bone and Xerxes had the spine of a jellyfish. But nothing could prepare us for the nonchalant decision to engage in ethnic cleansing.

> The king agreed . . . telling him, "Keep the money, but go ahead and do as you like with these people—whatever you think best."
>
> Two or three weeks later, Haman called in the king's secretaries

and dictated letters to the governors and officials throughout the empire, to each province in its own languages and dialects; these letters were signed in the name of King Ahasuerus and sealed with his ring. . . .

The edict went out by the king's speediest couriers. . . . Then the king and Haman sat down for a drinking spree as the city fell into confusion and panic. (vv. 10–12, 15 TLB)

The king and his right-hand man had such disregard for human life and disdain for the Jewish people that they could pronounce a bloodbath and then enjoy cocktails.

Note it wasn't just the Jews who were bewildered; the entire city was on edge. For all they knew Haman might turn on them. What if he had a bias against shop owners or farmers or people who were left handed? When the sheriff is a wimp and his deputy is a despot, anything can happen.

Haman dispatched couriers to each of the provinces with a command and an offer. The command? Kill all Jews. The offer? Plunder their possessions. The date dictated by the casting of the die was still eleven months away. *Let them live in misery*, Haman must have thought. What Haman did not know is this: "People throw lots to make a decision, but the answer comes from the LORD" (Prov. 16:33 NCV).

Chance didn't determine the date; God did. Even though this story does not mention his name, it reveals his will. It was God who delayed the date for eleven months, giving his plan time to unfold. It was God who reminded Mordecai of his ancestry, his identity. And it was God who prompted him to take a stand for what is right.

God will give you the courage to do the same.

Can we talk honestly for a moment? You are weary, wounded, and worried. Weary of the struggle, wounded from the battle, and worried that this winter will never cease. Like Mordecai and Esther, you feel far from home. Someone cut the ropes to the dock and set you adrift.

Persia can be a cruddy place. No one disagrees with that. But Persia can also be the petri dish for bad decisions. So I urge you, don't make matters worse by bowing before Haman.

Living as a person of faith in a faithless world requires courage and acts of resistance. You won't be told to kneel before a Persian tyrant. Odds are slim that you'll be persecuted by ISIS. But chances are high that you'll be tempted to compromise your beliefs or to remain silent in the face of injustice and evil. Mordecai moments are coming your way.

- Your college professor has a reputation for making fun of Christians. A few days before Easter he goes on a rant about the folly of the Christian faith. "No one in this class really believes that Jesus rose from the dead, right? Raise your hand if you do." How will you respond?
- You've been away from your family for a month. This overseas assignment is good for your career but rough on your marriage. Phone chats with your husband are tense. He's distant. You are lonely. One of your coworkers is attractive, attentive, and available. He made that clear today at work. His text just made it clear again. "Can I come over?" What will you tell him?
- As you are enjoying a burger with your bowling buddies, one of them tells a joke that makes fun of African Americans. You've never thought your friends were racists, but they all have a good laugh at this insensitive story. Will you laugh with them?
- You are the newcomer to the sales team. Job opportunities are scarce, and you don't want to mess up this one. The other members welcome you with a dinner invitation. You are surprised to hear them talk about the way they pad their expense accounts. "We don't get caught," one explains, "because we all agree to do it. You'll agree as well, won't you?" Everyone turns and awaits your reply. What will you say?

Living as a person

of faith in a faithless

world requires courage

and acts of resistance.

Mordecai moments. Instances in which our true allegiance is revealed. Everyone else bows, but what about you?

Mordecai had a few options. He could have said, "I'll bow on the outside but not on the inside." Or he could have justified going along in exchange for moving up. Or he could do what he did. He took a stand.

Can I urge you to do the same?

Resistance matters.

Long after acts of compliance are forgotten, acts of courage are pondered. Consider the now-famous photo of the man who refused to salute Hitler. No one captured the defiance of Mordecai on canvas. But the crossed arms of August Landmesser? Study the black-and-white photo taken at a 1936 Nazi rally in Hamburg, Germany, and you'll see him standing in a sea of Nazi loyalists. Hitler was present to christen a navy vessel. Hundreds of arms are extended in his direction. Everyone offers the "*Sieg Heil.*"

Except one. Twenty-six-year-old Landmesser was the lone German worker who refused to salute.

He wasn't always a dissident. He initially identified himself as a member of the Nazi Party. For two years he displayed no disloyalty. But then he met Irma Eckler in 1933. Their love story had one drawback. Eckler was Jewish. The party revoked his membership and denied him a marriage license.

In late 1935 the couple had a child. By the time the 1936 photo was taken, Hitler's anti-Semitism was well known. Is it any wonder that Landmesser refused to salute? He had fallen in love with a Jewish woman, been refused the right to marry her, and fathered a half-Jewish daughter.

The couple tried to leave Germany for Denmark in 1937. He was detained at the border for "dishonoring the race." Authorities told Landmesser to stop seeing Eckler, which he refused to do. Both were arrested in 1938. He was sent to a concentration camp. She went to prison, where she gave birth to their second daughter.

They never saw each other again. She died in 1942. He was drafted for the war in 1944, shortly after which he was declared MIA.[5]

Was it worth it? The fact that we are discussing his story provides a partial answer. No one finds courage in the sight of the saluting crowd. But who isn't inspired by the person who follows his or her convictions?

Landmesser crossed his arms.

The Egyptian Christians didn't disavow their faith.

Mordecai refused to bow.

And you? Mordecai's refusal to bow was the first link in a chain of courageous acts that led to the salvation of his people. Your resolve might be the decisive gesture that breaks the stronghold.

Decide now what you will do then.

Don't wait until the heat of the moment. A crisis is no time to prepare an escape plan. Being in the arms of your date in a motel room is not the time or place to make up your mind about morality. The day of your final exams is not the time to decide about honesty.

> The time to determine to resist temptation is before it strikes.

There is a reason the airline attendant points out the emergency exits before the plane leaves the ground. We don't think clearly during a free fall. The time to determine to resist temptation is before it strikes.

Mordecai not only refused to bow, but he determined he would never bow under any circumstances. The verse is written in the future tense rather than past. The future tense implies a resolve never to change his mind, regardless of the reaction of Haman.[6] Similarly Job resolved: "I made a covenant with my eyes not to look lustfully at a young woman" (Job 31:1). And Daniel "purposed in his heart that he would not defile himself" (Dan. 1:8 NKJV).

Make up your mind now about what you will do then. And remember:

Stand up for God, and he will stand with you.

A century and a half earlier three other Hebrews refused to bow as well. King Nebuchadnezzar of Babylon made an image of gold, ninety feet tall and nine feet wide, and commanded every citizen to bow before it (Dan. 3:1).

> Then the herald loudly proclaimed, "Nations and peoples of every language, this is what you are commanded to do: As soon as you hear the sound of the horn, flute, zither, lyre, harp, pipe and all kinds of music, you must fall down and worship the image of gold that King Nebuchadnezzar has set up. Whoever does not fall down and worship will immediately be thrown into a blazing furnace." (vv. 4–6)

That is an interesting church-growth strategy. Come to worship, or we'll toast you like a marshmallow. Everyone complied, except three Jews. The king was given this report:

> "But there are some Jews whom you have set over the affairs of the province of Babylon—Shadrach, Meshach and Abednego—who pay no attention to you, Your Majesty. They neither serve your gods nor worship the image of gold you have set up."
>
> Furious with rage, Nebuchadnezzar summoned Shadrach, Meshach and Abednego. . . . "If you are ready to fall down and worship the image I made, very good. But if you do not worship it, you will be thrown immediately into a blazing furnace. Then what god will be able to rescue you from my hand?"
>
> Shadrach, Meshach and Abednego replied to him, "King Nebuchadnezzar, we do not need to defend ourselves before you in this matter." (Dan. 3:12–13, 15–16)

This stuff happens in exile. No matter how much wisdom and tact you have, how humble you are, how graciously you hold your convictions, and how many times you've refused to fight about something, there will come a time when your faith will be under fire. You'll be asked to do something that is wrong.

Shadrach, Meshach, and Abednego did not waver.

Nebuchadnezzar went ballistic and ordered that the furnace be heated to seven times its typical temperature. The heat was so intense that the soldiers who bound the Hebrews were consumed by the blazing furnace. Nebuchadnezzar, with morbid fascination, positioned himself at the furnace entrance. He wanted to watch the Hebrews sizzle. Yet he saw something else entirely.

> Then King Nebuchadnezzar leaped to his feet in amazement and asked his advisers, "Weren't there three men that we tied up and threw into the fire?"
>
> They replied, "Certainly, Your Majesty."
>
> He said, "Look! I see four men walking around in the fire, unbound and unharmed, and the fourth looks like a son of the gods." (vv. 24–25)

Not only were the three men untouched by the flames, but there was also a fourth man, who had a divine appearance! Was this the Son of God? Certainly seems to be the case. Jesus stood with those who stood for him.

The Hebrew trio marched out of the fire with greater impact than when they entered. Nebuchadnezzar had no interest in their faith prior to the furnace. But then he saw that the "fire had not harmed their bodies, nor was a hair of their heads singed; their robes were not scorched, and there was no smell of fire on them. Then Nebuchadnezzar said, 'Praise be to the God of Shadrach, Meshach and Abednego, who has sent his angel and rescued his servants!'" (vv. 27–28).

The attempts of the devil backfired. They did then; they do still.

Consider the story of the martyrs in Libya in 2015. There is some evidence that one of the men did not walk onto the beach as a Christian.

> Courage is contagious.

Unlike the others he was not from Egypt; he was a citizen of Ghana. It was not until he saw the faith of the men around him that he was moved to trust in Christ. When the time came to make his decision, asked whether he would denounce Christianity and live or proclaim the gospel and die, he said, "Their God is my God."[7]

Courage is contagious. My prayer is that your courage will inspire the same in others.

Chapter Five

RELIEF WILL COME

As far as rescue stories go, mine is wimpy. It won't be made into a movie. I was never interviewed by a media outlet. You'll never read my story in *National Geographic* or *Reader's Digest*. In the encyclopedia of rescue operations, mine wouldn't warrant a footnote. Yet what was no news to others was big news to the three of us who got plucked out of the cold prairie.

We were college students earning extra cash during Christmas break by working in the oil field. It was a blustery, bitter, extra-set-of-long-johns December day. In the oil patch food chain, part-time college kids ranked somewhere near pond scum. Roustabouts were unimpressed with smooth-skinned students who showed up for a couple of weeks and could hardly tell a broom from a shovel. Consequently, any particularly dirty job was handed to us.

That day's dirty job was a ditch that needed to be dug some twenty miles from the nearest sign of civilization. The boss drove us out, dropped us off, and left us with a promise to return at 5:00 p.m. The terrain was skillet-pan flat. The wind was bone-chilling cold. We pulled our wool caps over our ears and our jacket collars up around our necks and got to work. By quitting time we were frozen, tired, and tired of being frozen.

We set our shovels on the ground and looked down the dirt road. We longed for a ride home in a warm truck. We saw no one. Five thirty, no truck. The sun set, the chill factor dipped into single digits, and still no sign of anyone. We had no cell phone or GPS system. My college years were just barely out of the Stone Age. We were marooned.

Turns out the person slated to fetch us had forgotten us. Sunset became nightfall. Stars began to appear, and coyotes began to howl. Our hands were numb. Our cheeks were icy. Our situation was desperate.

Know the feeling? Mordecai did.

By the time we get to this point in the story, Haman had convinced the easily convinceable Xerxes to destroy all the Jews. The dice have been cast, the date of death has been set, and the decree has gone to all corners of Persia. Mordecai got word of the impending holocaust and abandoned all pretense.

> When Mordecai learned of all that had been done, he tore his clothes, put on sackcloth and ashes, and went out into the city, wailing loudly and bitterly. But he went only as far as the king's gate, because no one clothed in sackcloth was allowed to enter it. (Est. 4:1–2)

News of the extermination decree drove Mordecai into a state of anguish. He wardrobed himself in coarse cloth and smeared his face with soot and ashes. He donned the garb of a funeral dirge. He roamed the streets of Susa, crying, screaming, and beating his chest. Officials stopped and stared. Store owners turned and watched. What a spectacle! Remember, he was known for his importance to the queen, a courtier in the gate. Yet Mordecai breached all decorum.

Esther got word of the wailing and was aghast that he would behave in such a manner. So she sent him a batch of clothing and told him in no uncertain terms to quit throwing such a fit. He was jeopardizing everything the two had put in place. They had won favor with the king and respect in the citadel. Apparently she was unaware of the decree, an indication of how cloistered she was from public life.

What followed was a flurry of couriered messages between the two. Mordecai sent Esther a copy of the extermination orders and urged her to reach out to her husband, the king.

A queen can't just saunter into the throne room, she reminded Mordecai. If she showed up uninvited, a cranky king could have her head.

> All the king's officials and the people of the royal provinces know that for any man or woman who approaches the king in the inner court without being summoned the king has but one law: that they be put to death unless the king extends the gold scepter to them and spares their lives. But thirty days have passed since I was called to go to the king. (v. 11)

Can't we envision Esther ticking off on her fingers the reasons to stay silent?

It is against the law.

It's been thirty days since he gave me so much as a second look.

The king's in a foul mood, for sure.

He will probably kill me. Remember Vashti?

Mordecai gave her reservations some thought and sent a message.

Before we read his words, can I tee them up? They are some of the most profound observations you will read in the Bible. What he said in two verses is worth two volumes of consideration. Mordecai the Jew became Mordecai the theologian. He made a declaration that reveals the heart of a person who has encountered the heart of the holy God. You are about to hear the greatest one-paragraph call to courage ever spoken by a human tongue.

Have I sufficiently raised your expectations? See if you don't agree:

> Do not think that because you are in the king's house you alone of all the Jews will escape. For if you remain silent at this time, relief and deliverance for the Jews will arise from another place,

but you and your father's family will perish. And who knows but that you have come to your royal position for such a time as this? (vv. 13–14)

How do we survive the bitterly cold winds of life? When the downsizing has been declared. When the pandemic has no vaccine. When the account has no cash. When the marriage has no joy. When the crib is empty or the grave is occupied or the double bed is down to you, and you can't quit crying yourself to sleep.

When circumstances leave you desperate and feeling all alone in a wintry ditch, might Mordecai's words be worth the retelling? He made a duo of starchy observations.

No one gets a free pass.

Not even the queen of Persia. "Do not think that because you are in the king's house you alone of all the Jews will escape." Don't think for a second, Esther, that you'll get through the genocide unscathed. The fact that the Jews will be saved in no way assures that you and the good name of your father's house will survive. Your legacy will be sacrificed on the altar of apathy. You might dodge the first bullet, but there are five more in the clip. Trouble knocks at the door of us all.

"Gee, thanks, Max. You call this good news? I thought you were going to give me some hope to help me get through this tough time."

Maybe you didn't need the reminder, but someone does. Someone has been led to believe that the Christian life is a yellow-brick road and a trip home to Kansas is only a click of the ruby reds away. Consequently when the inevitable bad stuff happens, the person is forced to face not just the bad stuff but also the tough questions about a God who didn't keep his promises. To which God says, "I never made those promises."

Here is what God said: "In this world you will have trouble" (John 16:33). You will, at times, feel as though you've received "the sentence of death" (2 Cor. 1:9 ESV). You will "pass through the waters . . . pass through the rivers . . . walk through the fire" (Isa. 43:2).

Troubles come with life. We gain nothing by pretending they don't. No one gets a free pass, but one way or another *relief and deliverance will come.*

Relief came our way that evening on the Texas prairie. We'd just about talked ourselves into beginning the hike home when we saw the most wondrous of sights: headlights. Tiny at first, bouncing up and down like a waving flashlight. When we saw the headlights, everything changed. We were still cold. Still tired. The truck was still in the distance. The night was still dark. But the sight of headlights gave us hope.

Mordecai saw something similar. Bouncing headlights appeared on his horizon. In the beginning of chapter 4, we saw him lamenting in the streets, expecting disaster. When he learned of the order to kill all the Jews, "he tore his clothes, put on sackcloth and ashes, and went out into the city, wailing loudly and bitterly" (Est. 4:1). This was a ferocious image: threads ripping, throat screaming, garments torn, flesh exposed. To tear clothing was to declare outwardly what was happening inwardly. Mordecai was all torn up inside. Of this we can be certain: he was desperate. Thirteen verses later he made an about-face and told Esther, "Relief and deliverance will arise for the Jews" (v. 14 NKJV).

What happened to him? Why the change from desperate to bold? Here is my best guess. God awakened a suppressed belief. On Mordecai's mama's knee he'd been told how Moses and a million Hebrews had an angry sea on one side and an angry Pharaoh on the other, how a shepherd boy stood waist high with a Goliath of a giant, how Daniel could hear the growling of the lions and the growling of their tummies. But then God spoke up. The sea opened up, David rose up, and the lions shut up!

It dawned on Mordecai that the God of Abraham, Isaac, and

Jacob was alive and well and undefeated in battle. The Jews were far from Jerusalem, but they were not far from God. Mordecai may have neglected his role as a curator of the covenant, but God had not forgotten his role as a covenant keeper. God's heart was still attached to his people—a remnant carried away from Zion and living in exile in Persia. The Jews had no king, no army, no temple, no priesthood, no sacrifices. No matter. They still had their Jehovah. Not once was God threatened, undone, bewildered, or befuddled. God is to problems what a hurricane is to a mosquito. No match. Mordecai got this.

Do you? Do you get this? Do you know the rest of the verses?

"In this world you will have trouble. But take heart!" declared Jesus. "I have overcome the world." (John 16:33)

Indeed, we felt that we had received the sentence of death. But that was to make us rely not on ourselves but on God who raises the dead. (2 Cor. 1:9 ESV)

Yes, the journey ahead includes waters and rivers and fires. But . . .

> When you pass through the waters, I will be with you;
> and through the rivers, they shall not overwhelm you;
> when you walk through fire you shall not be burned,
> and the flame shall not consume you.
>
> (ISA. 43:2 ESV)

Does your view of God include a certain relief and a dramatic deliverance? That is no small question. Indeed, that is *the* question. The vast majority of people see no pending relief. Their summary of life reads like a Shakespearean tragedy. "We live in a beautiful but broken world. It cannot be fixed. Nothing can be done. We make the best of it and then die." For many people that's life in a nutshell. So it's hardly any surprise that we live in a day marked by despair and suicide.

The story God offers is, by comparison, a golden meadow. It begins like the other but ends in a far better place.

"We live in a beautiful but broken world. However, our Creator made this world and did not destine it or us for brokenness. He destined us for a wonderful life. His intentions for us are good. He cares so much for us that he became one of us. He took on our brokenness, even to the point of death. His death gave birth to our life—eternal life. He arose from the dead and is recreating our world and invites all of us to be a part of it. One day he will restore the world to its intended beauty and reclaim his family, and we will live with him forever."

This was the message of Mordecai: *Relief is coming.*

And then he said to Esther, "Who knows but that you have come to your royal position for such a time as this?" (Est. 4:14).

Esther's response was significant.

> Go, gather together all the Jews who are in Susa, and fast for me. Do not eat or drink for three days, night or day. I and my attendants will fast as you do. When this is done, I will go to the king, even though it is against the law. And if I perish, I perish. (v. 16)

You just read the turning point in the development of our main character. The faith of Hadassah merges with the authority of the crown. She commands Mordecai (in the imperative, with no polite circumlocutions) to assemble the Jews in Susa for a public fast. In doing so she assumes the role of a moral leader for her people. Resolve replaces passivity. She is no longer the beauty queen. She is a woman of God, determined to lead her people through a crisis.

What happened? What moved Esther from "I can't do anything" to "I'm willing to lose everything"? What took her from "If I go, I'll perish" to "If I perish, I perish"?

This is your moment.

You were made to

stand up like Mordecai,

to speak up like Esther.

It had to be the straightforward message of Mordecai. Yes, the world is in a mess. Yes, we've fallen victim to a brutal Haman. But relief will come, and "who knows whether you have come to the kingdom for such a time as this?" (v. 14 NKJV). Mordecai opened a window and shed a divine light into Esther's world. "You are here for a reason," he said. "Your life is part of a plan. You were placed here on purpose for a purpose."

So were you, my friend. You, like Esther, were made for this moment. To be clear, you didn't ask for this struggle. You want to get past it. You don't know how much longer you can hold up.

But what if God is in this? Did he not place you on this planet in this generation? He determined your birth date and nationality and selected your neighborhood (Acts 17:26). What if you, like Esther, have an opportunity to act in a way that will bless more people than you could imagine?

This is your hour. This is your moment. You were made to stand up like Mordecai, to speak up like Esther.

Deliverance will come. God will have his victory. He will rescue his people. He will right the wrongs of this world. The question is not, Will God prevail? The question is, Will you be part of the team?

Had Esther remained silent, she would have missed the opportunity to save thousands of her kin. God would have delivered his children through someone else. As Mordecai cautioned, "Relief and deliverance for the Jews will arise from another place, but you and your father's family will perish" (Est. 4:14). Perhaps she hoped this turmoil would

> The question is not, Will God prevail? The question is, Will you be part of the team?

pass her by. She may have considered silencing Mordecai. She was the queen, after all. Her Jewish ancestry was still a secret. Isolation was a sure temptation. Yet Mordecai cautioned strongly against it. Inaction would be costly. Esther's name and the name of her family would have become bywords for apathy.

What about you and me? We can retreat if we want. Let our hearts grow hard, our faith grow cold. Hibernate. Hide out. Go dark. Stay quiet. Or we can see our challenge as an opportunity to join God in his work.

This was the choice that faced Martin Luther King Jr. late one evening in January 1956. At the tender age of twenty-seven, he took up the cause that would lead to a boycott and the civil rights movement. Less than a week after Rosa Parks refused to give up her seat on a bus to a white passenger, King became president of the Montgomery Improvement Association of Montgomery, Alabama.

He immediately began receiving death threats. One phone call in particular left him unnerved. In a speech he later recounted, "On the other end was an ugly voice. That voice said to me, in substance, 'N---r, we are tired of you and your mess now. And if you aren't out of this town in three days, we're going to blow your brains out and blow up your house.'"

King stepped into his kitchen to regather his thoughts. He considered his beautiful wife and precious little girl. He imagined the rage that awaited him in the streets. He questioned whether the effort was worth the risk.

He considered calling his father or mother. But he chose to do something else. "Something said to me, you can't call on Daddy now, he's up in Atlanta a hundred and seventy-five miles away. You can't even call on Mama now. You've got to call on that something in that person that your Daddy used to tell you about. That power that can make a way out of no way."

King bowed his head and asked God for help. "And it seemed at that moment that I could hear an inner voice saying to me, 'Martin Luther, stand up for righteousness, stand up for justice, stand up for truth. And lo I will be with you, even until the end of the world.'"

Freshly fortified, King continued the work, leaving his mark on what is arguably the most prominent movement of the twentieth century. Even so, he continued to struggle with fear for the rest of his life. In the speech in which he shared the story of the kitchen, he admitted, "Living every day under extensive criticisms, even from Negroes, I feel discouraged sometimes . . . and feel my work's in vain. But then the Holy Spirit revives my soul again."[1]

> Relief will come. May God help you and me to be a part of it.

Each of our lives intersects with opportunities in which we can come alongside the work of God. We won't speak to a Persian king. Very few will lead a movement of liberty. But heaven will offer each one of us, without exception, the privilege of participating in holy work.

When your invitation comes, may you hear the same Spirit that Reverend King heard, find the same courage Esther found, and make the same decision Mordecai made. Relief will come. May God help you and me to be a part of it.

Chapter Six

TWO THRONE ROOMS

S everal films have been based on the story of Esther. In the ones I have seen, she is ravishingly gorgeous. Eyes shaped like crescents, unblemished olive skin. A Hollywood heartthrob, this lady. And, indeed, she must have been. Selected as the queen of Persia out of a harem of lovely contenders.

The movies are equally unanimous as to the moment of high drama: Esther and her unsolicited visit to King Xerxes. She stands at the throne room entryway, robed in elegance. The camera can hardly bear to turn away from her splendor. When it does, we see Xerxes wide-eyed with mouth open. "What can I do for you, my beauty?" The implied message of the movies is clear: the good looks of Esther softened and swayed the hard heart of Xerxes.

Yet Scripture tells a different story. Yes, she appeared before the king. Yes, she did so at great risk. And, yes, Xerxes lowered his scepter and invited her to enter. But it wasn't her beauty that made the difference. Look at the text, and see if you agree.

Then Esther sent this reply to Mordecai: "Go, gather together all the Jews who are in Susa, and fast for me. Do not eat or drink for three days, night or day. I and my attendants will fast as you do. When this is done, I will go to the king, even though it is against the law. And if I perish, I perish." (Est. 4:15–16)

She realized, perhaps for the first time, that silence is a form of acquiescence. Her people, the Jews, had been declared worthy of mass murder, and she has done nothing. Either she was too oblivious to know or too afraid to act. Either way, her apathy was inexcusable.

But what could she do? The king had made his decision. The vizier had declared the death penalty. Neither had any interest in a change of mind. Just the opposite. They were making a statement: don't mess with Xerxes. Esther faced an immovable wall and the possibility of death for making the wrong move. She responded, not with a call to her hair stylist, but with a retreat into the prayer chamber.

Rather than rush into the throne room of Xerxes, she humbled herself and stepped into the throne room of God.

In the movie I wish someone would make, Esther reads the words of Mordecai and crumbles into a heap, face-first on the floor of her bedroom. Her nation is about to be led to slaughter. It's going to be a bloodbath, and she sleeps with the king who ordered it. Her handmaids see her fall to the ground and rush to her aid. She waves them away. "Just get word to Mordecai: I'll go to see the king. Even if it costs me my life. Tell everyone to pray."

This is a new Esther. Until this point she had relied on her good looks. Now she casts herself upon her God.

She will soon stand before Xerxes. She will soon risk her life. She will seek the reversal of an irreversible law that has been sponsored by the most powerful man in the empire and endorsed with the king's own signet ring. She knows that God's intervention is their only hope. This is a prayer of desperation.

Three days. No food. No water. Fears took her sleep. Hunger gnawed at her gut. Dehydration dried her skin and hollowed her eyes. She prayed a prayer of tears.

You know what happened next. When Esther entered the king's throne room, she was once again a head-to-toe picture of Persian perfection. One look at her and the jaw of Xerxes hit the ground. The scripture says, "he was pleased with her and held out to her the gold scepter that was in his hand" (5:2).

Pleased with her? How about "unraveled by her"? "Overwhelmed by her"? "Reduced to ice cream on a July sidewalk by the sight of her"? "I'll give you half of the kingdom," the king gulped. He was a middle schooler; she was a college-age cheerleader. I get that.

But it wasn't her glamour that opened the throne room door. It was her prayers. She came before the king in beauty only after she lingered before the King of kings in humility. Aren't we called to do the same?

Don't think for a moment that you have what it takes to weather this winter. Yet don't think for a second that God won't give you what you need.

Many years ago when our family lived in Brazil, a new Christian came to one of our church leaders with a question. He'd been reading his Bible (good for him), and he discovered this promise: "Whatever things you ask in prayer, believing, you will receive" (Matt. 21:22 NKJV).

"Does our church believe this passage?" he wondered.

What is a missionary to say? "Yes, of course."

"Then," he posed, "why do we work so hard and pray so little?"

Good question. Why do we? What if the only thing between you and a season of refreshing is prayer? I don't mean a shallow tip o' the hat to the "man upstairs." I'm talking about heartfelt prayer. I can't think of a more simple—or more important—way that we can partner with God in bringing about a reversal.

Searching for springtime? You don't need more advice from your fishing buddies. You don't need the ten easy steps to happiness as advertised on the cover of a tabloid. You don't need another psychobabble talk show. You need the tool that Esther found, that Daniel found. You need to pray.

Daniel was a young man when he was taken into Babylonian

Don't think for a moment
that you have what it takes to
weather this winter. Yet don't
think for a second that God
won't give you what you need.

captivity in 605 BC. Later in his life he came to an understanding of the future of his people. He realized that the seventy years of prophesied captivity were coming to an end. He took the matter to the Lord.

> So listen, God, to this determined prayer of your servant. Have mercy on your ruined Sanctuary. Act out of who you are, not out of what we are.
>
> Turn your ears our way, God, and listen. Open your eyes and take a long look at our ruined city, this city named after you. We know that we don't deserve a hearing from you. Our appeal is to your compassion. This prayer is our last and only hope. (Dan. 9:17–18 THE MESSAGE)

What word describes the tone of Daniel's prayer? *Eloquence? Authority?* Lofty *poetry?* I don't think so either. How about this word: *humility?*

"Have mercy," he begged.

"Act out of who you are, not out of what we are."

"We don't deserve a hearing from you."

"Our appeal is to your compassion."

Daniel threw himself on the mercy of the highest court.

If any person deserved to be heard by God, it was he. Scripture portrays him as a man beyond reproach. There is no hint of adultery, rebellion, or infidelity. In Scripture he was a holy man. Yet in the presence of God, this holy man offered a brokenhearted prayer.

The prayer so moved the heart of God that an angel was sent with a message.

> From the moment you decided to humble yourself to receive understanding, your prayer was heard, and I set out to come to you. But I was waylaid by the angel-prince of the kingdom of Persia and was delayed for a good three weeks. But then Michael, one of the chief

angel-princes, intervened to help me. I left him there with the prince of the kingdom of Persia. And now I'm here to help you. (Dan. 10:12–14 THE MESSAGE)

The angel came to help when Daniel knelt and prayed.

The moment you bow your head to pray is the moment God lifts his hand to help. Your heavenly Father wants to hear from you. Desperate? Without options? Without solutions? By no means. Now more than ever is the time to get down on your knees and plead for mercy.

That's the situation I found myself in during the summer of 2020. The year had taken its toll on us all. The world was whipsawed by the presence of a pandemic, the absence of a vaccine. The White House was in turmoil, and the job market was in shambles. And, as if we needed another tsunami, a Black man in Minneapolis died at the hands of a White police officer, and the rage erupted. Anger poured into city streets from New York to Portland.

In San Antonio, the city where I have pastored since 1988, a group of us chose to call people to prayer. We rented the city's largest parking lot. We designed banners and organized a prayer service. We decided to follow the example of Mordecai and Esther and pray for God's help. We also resolved to repent. "If my people, who are called by my name, will humble themselves and pray and seek my face and *turn from their wicked ways,* then I will hear from heaven, and I will forgive their sin and will heal their land" (2 Chron. 7:14, emphasis mine).

There must be a turning from wicked ways, a repentance of sin.

But what sin, Lord? we wondered. *There are so many.* Then, in as clear a word as I have ever heard from God, the answer came: the sin of racism. Our nation needs to repent for the

> The moment you bow your head to pray is the moment God lifts his hand to help.

centuries of oppression that we have imposed on our Black brothers and sisters.

As it turned out, I oversaw this citywide prayer. I was unenthused at the idea of leading a prayer of repentance for this transgression. My excuses were abundant, and I made sure heaven heard them all. "But I'm not a racist. I've done nothing wrong against the Black community. I've never spoken against African Americans."

But you've never spoken up for them, either. Another clear word from the Father.

I recalled how Daniel made his appeal, how Mordecai went public with his lament, how Esther refused to speak to the king until she had spoken to the King.

I asked a Black pastor to join me on the platform. With thousands watching in person and tens of thousands online, I knelt at the altar and repented as he stood beside me.

Father, you have made from one blood every nation of men and women to dwell on the face of the earth. We are all of one blood. There is no Black blood. There is no White blood. There is no Brown blood. There is no Asian blood. There is only one blood.

When you died, you shed your precious blood so all people of all nations could be saved. This was, and is, your plan. They are all precious in your sight. Yet they have not been precious in ours.

For that sin, O Lord, we are sorry.

I, Max Lucado, am sorry. I am sorry that I have been silent. My head has been buried in the sand. My brothers and sisters are hurting on the side of the road, and I have walked a wide circle to avoid them. I have made them feel less than. I did not realize their trauma.

I am sorry.

We are sorry. Our ancestors were wrong. When they bought and sold people, that was wrong. When they claimed superiority over Black people, that was wrong. When they refused to share water fountains, city buses, and restaurants with your children, that was a sin.

For the occasions that your church has broken your heart by refusing entrance to your children of color, we beg your mercy. We agree with you: that was wrong.

Heal this land, O Lord. You can do what policies and politicians cannot. You can break down the walls of bias and prejudice. Please, in the name of Jesus, do so today.

Did the prayer prompt a national renewal? I can't say that it did. But the prayer prompted a young African American woman to say to me, "That's all I needed to hear to keep from giving up."

Are you, like Esther, facing an impossible challenge? Then imitate the queen.

Esther could have remained hidden and done nothing. Or she could have rushed into the presence of Xerxes. But she chose the wiser recourse. She chose prayer. Her story urges us to do the same.

This is the time for a no-nonsense, honest, face-on-the-floor talk with the Lord of All. Garments need not be ripped, but veneer must be removed. Three days of fasting is optional, but the prayer of genuine humility is not.

What is your version of Xerxes? What Haman-sized challenge are you facing? Is your job in jeopardy? Is your loved one in hospice? Is your family under attack? Is your faith in tatters? Retreat into your prayer closet.

The queen could enter the throne room of Xerxes because she had spent time in the throne room of God. The same is true in your story and mine. Once we've spoken to the King of heaven, we are ready to face any king on earth.

ACT 3
CONQUEST

THE HAND OF GOD IN THE DETAILS OF HISTORY

Mordecai was dreaming. In his sleep he saw Esther as a child running down a grassy hill into his arms. Her hair flew in black ribbons behind her. Her laughter made the meadowlarks jealous. He swept her up until she was high enough to eclipse the after-noon sun.

In the dream she called him Abba, and even though he wasn't, he was the only father she'd ever known. He lowered her to the ground and was about to chase her through the meadow when . . .

"Wake up, Mordecai."

He kept his eyes shut and his chin on his chest. He didn't want to wake up.

"You can't sit here like a beggar."

Mordecai blinked. The light of the moon illuminated the silent street. He felt the hard wall behind his back and the cobbled path beneath his rear. He lifted his head.

"Hegai?"

"Yes," replied his friend.

"I must have dozed," he mumbled through dry lips.

"It is almost dawn."

"I slept all night?"

"Yes, you are weary. You've been fasting for three days. Let me get you something to eat."

Mordecai pushed himself to his feet. "Not yet. Not until I hear from the queen."

His head felt light. He leaned back against the wall. His goat-hair robe scratched his skin.

"That's why I'm here. She wants to see you."

"The queen?"

"Yes, come with me."

Mordecai placed a hand on Hegai's shoulder and followed close behind. The courtyard was empty except for a few guards. They looked bored. As the two men stepped through an archway, Hegai threw an embroidered robe over his friend's shoulders. Mordecai did not object. He would not be allowed into the gate wearing his humble robe of repentance.

Soon they came to a large door. Hegai pulled it open, and they stepped inside. Hegai waited by the door as Mordecai walked into the room. Small lamps gave enough light to reveal a large table. Unlit torches were evenly spaced on the walls. A hearth sat at the end, its fire reduced to embers. Mordecai knew this banquet room well. Only a week ago he might have been here feasting and laughing with an entourage of partiers.

But all that changed when he disclosed his ethnicity and took up sackcloth and ashes. For days he had wandered through the streets of the capital. His cries echoed among the arches and parapets. His days as a diplomat were over. The days of the Jews were numbered. They needed someone to plead their case before the king. That "someone" was standing near the end of the long table, awaiting him.

He walked as near to her as protocol permitted and lowered his head.

He then lifted it to see her face, tear-streaked. Her lips were dry and chapped. She wore only a simple dress.

"I am ready," she said. Her voice was steady, resolute, brave.

"You will go to the king? Unsolicited?"

"Yes."

"If he receives you, be direct with him."

"No, I must be subtle."

Mordecai tilted his head in question.

"He knows only the language of pleasure. I will speak it."

She whispered her plans. He nodded. "That is wise." He then told her, "I visited the village of the Jews several times during these last days. They are praying. Even the children."

The queen smiled at the thought.

"The children?"

"Yes. They gave me a divine message to share with you."

"A divine message?"

"They stopped me on the street and cited it. 'Be not afraid of the sudden terror, neither of the destruction of the wicked when it comes.'"[1]

Esther nodded. "May it be so. May their prayers rise to heaven."

Then for a long moment, silence.

She extended her hand, so soft and clean. He took it in his.

"Abba?"

"My child?"

"If I perish ... what then?"

Mordecai swallowed hard and sighed. "If you perish, you will see your mother, your father. Abraham will greet you. Ruth will welcome you ..."

"And what about our people?"

"God will yet deliver them."

She nodded as he spoke. Candlelight reflected in her now-moist eyes.

For a moment she was not the queen. He was not a nobleman. Their people were not under a sentence of death.

The two were in the field, a field of gold.

Hegai stepped into the light. "My queen, it's time," he interrupted.

And with that she was gone.

Chapter Seven

GOD IS LOUDEST WHEN HE WHISPERS

I find no comfort in the butterfly effect. It offers me no solace to ponder its possibility. Do you know the theory of which I speak? The butterfly effect traces the existence of a hurricane in Florida to a busy insect in West Africa.[1] It goes something like this: A butterfly flaps its wings at just the right time and stirs the smallest of air gusts. The burst of air grows and grows, rippling around the globe until it results in a chaotic storm.

I'm on board with the butterfly part. The idea that small things lead to big events? No one who has planted a seed can dispute the power of modest beginnings. It's not the result I question; it's the randomness. Are humans the victims of wing flaps? Do entire cities wash out to sea because an insect is active? Are we nothing more than weather vanes whipped about by faceless fate? Who finds consolation in a philosophy of happenstance and accidents?

I don't, but I do find great comfort in promises like these:

Our God is in the heavens, and he does as he wishes. (Ps. 115:3 NLT)

From eternity to eternity I am God. No one can oppose what I do. (Isa. 43:13 TLB)

We were chosen from the beginning to be [God's], and all things happen just as he decided long ago. (Eph. 1:11 TLB)

One prophet asked, "Who can command things to happen without the Lord's permission?" (Lam. 3:37 NLT)

Another declared, "No one can interrupt his work, no one can call his rule into question." (Dan. 4:35 THE MESSAGE)

He declared: "I make known the end from the beginning, from ancient times, what is still to come. I say, 'My purpose will stand, and I will do all that I please.'" (Isa. 46:10)

The butterfly might stir, but only with the permission of God can a wing flap create a hurricane. He is "the blessed controller of all things." (1 Tim. 6:15 PHILLIPS)

He certainly was in the story of Esther. You might buckle your seatbelt. The next few scenes unfold at high speed. Chapter 5 opens with Esther re-robed in royalty and standing in the inner court just close enough for the king to catch a glimpse of his queen and a whiff of her perfume. "When he saw Queen Esther standing in the court, he was pleased with her and held out to her the gold scepter that was in his hand. So Esther approached and touched the tip of the scepter" (v. 2).

(I have it on good authority that when Xerxes held out his golden scepter, he was, in Persian parlance, saying, "Hey, good lookin'. Whatcha got cookin'?") Not only did he invite her to enter, but he also welcomed her petition. "What is it, Queen Esther? What is your request? Even up to half the kingdom, it will be given you" (v. 3).

Esther requested a dinner date. A nice evening that included the king, her, and Haman. Just the three of them, some chitchat, a bottle of bubbly, and a few Frank Sinatra songs. The quickest way to a man's heart is through his tummy, right?

The evening was a great success. Haman left with a full belly and a big head. Life was good. He was the king's in-house counsel and the queen's go-to guy for black-tie affairs. He smiled to himself as he strode through the palace courtyard, nodding at the row of subservient servants. Could life be sweeter? Then he saw Mordecai sitting at the gate, still wearing sackcloth and ashes, refusing to bow. Haman snarled.

Goodbye, good mood. Hello, grumps. Haman went home as cheerless as a marathoner with bunions. He gathered his friends and wife and told them, in no uncertain terms, that Mordecai was raining on his parade.

"I'm the only person Queen Esther invited to accompany the king to the banquet she gave. And she has invited me along with the king tomorrow. But all this gives me no satisfaction as long as I see that Jew Mordecai sitting at the king's gate."

His wife Zeresh and all his friends said to him, "Have a pole set up, reaching to a height of fifty cubits, and ask the king in the morning to have Mordecai impaled on it. Then go with the king to the banquet and enjoy yourself." This suggestion delighted Haman, and he had the pole set up. (vv. 12–14)

A surgical strike! Yes, that's it. Send the message loud and clear. Doom to all dissenters. Death to all the disobedient. Haman ordered the construction of gallows that measured seventy-five feet tall. That's seven and a half stories! Persian gallows did not include a rope around the neck but rather a stake thrust through the body. Haman went to bed that night thinking about Mordecai being skewered on a stick. Not the most pleasant way to fall asleep. But Haman was not a pleasant person.

Speaking of sleep, King Xerxes couldn't. He tossed and turned. He pounded his pillow and pounded it again. He sat on the edge of the bed, groaned, and belched. He blamed the sleeplessness on the spicy meat sauce. He'd have been wiser to blame it on heaven's butterfly.

Modern-day insomniacs listen to Lucado sermons for treatment. Xerxes had no such therapy, so he requested a (yawn) reading of the book of records. The court attendant entered the chamber carrying a fat scroll. He opened it and began to drone on and on and on. He read the minutes from the last council meeting in a flat, nasal tone that would have anesthetized a patient for bypass surgery.

"Six gates were ordered for Susa."

"The king approved new helmets for the army."

"Seven million paper clips were dispatched into the kingdom."

"Mordecai saved the king's life by reporting an assassination attempt."

What?! The king sat straight up in bed and told the reader, "Stop right there!"

Do you recall this moment from earlier in the story? Mordecai overheard two insurgents plotting to kill the king. He reported their scheme to Esther. The queen reported it to Xerxes. The king survived. The matter was recorded in the books, and nothing was done for Mordecai. Until now.

"'What honor and recognition has Mordecai received for this?' the king asked" (6:3).

When the king learned that nothing had been done to honor the man who had saved his life, he was apoplectic. How could this be? Mordecai, who had protected the crown, had received not so much as a gold watch. Xerxes climbed out of bed and began to pace. Something needed to be done. But what? Xerxes needed some advice.

> The king said, "Who is in the court?" Now Haman had just entered the outer court of the palace to speak to the king about impaling Mordecai on the pole he had set up for him.
>
> His attendants answered, "Haman is standing in the court."
>
> "Bring him in," the king ordered. (vv. 4–5)

It was the crack of dawn. Both men were in the royal palace with Mordecai on their minds. Xerxes wanted to honor him. Haman wanted to gore him.

The king called for Haman. Haman fluffed his peacock feathers and strutted into the king's quarters. But before he could say, "Top o' the morning," Xerxes asked him a question. "'What should be done for the man the king delights to honor?' Now Haman thought to himself, 'Who is there that the king would rather honor than me?'" (v. 6).

Narcissist that Haman was, he assumed the king was giving him props and being coy about it. After all, who was more worthy of royal recognition? He puffed on his fingernails and buffed them against his chest. He envisioned the day unfolding before him. He would ride astride the steed of the king, wearing the royal robe. People would pave his path with rose petals and bow as he passed. He would blow kisses, and they would reciprocate. It would be grand.

> So he answered the king, "For the man the king delights to honor, have them bring a royal robe the king has worn and a horse the king has ridden, one with a royal crest placed on its head. Then let the robe and horse be entrusted to one of the king's most noble princes. Let them robe the man the king delights to honor, and lead him on the horse through the city streets, proclaiming before him, 'This is what is done for the man the king delights to honor!'" (vv. 7–9)

"Great idea," said Xerxes the king.

Of course, it is, thought Haman the egomaniac.

What happened next is one of the great moments in the Bible. "'Go at once,' the king commanded Haman. 'Get the robe and the horse and do just as you have suggested for Mordecai the Jew, who sits at the king's gate. Do not neglect anything you have recommended'" (v. 10).

Could it get any better?

Within moments it was Mordecai Day in Susa, complete with a marching band full of Susa-phones. (Sorry, I tried to resist.) Behold the first of several reversals of fortune in this story. Haman intended to put Mordecai on a spike. Instead, Haman placed him on a horse. Haman planned to lead Mordecai to the gallows to the sound of jeers. Instead, he led him through the streets to the sound of cheers. Haman wanted the king to throw him a parade. Now he wanted to throw up.[2]

How do you say "poetic justice" in Persian?

After the celebration "Haman hurried home, mourning, with his head covered. And Haman informed Zeresh his wife and all his friends of everything that had happened to him" (vv. 12–13 NASB).

Who saw this coming? Who could have envisioned such a hairpin U-turn? The answer? God could!

God orchestrated all the details. The sleepless king. The detailed reading. The entry about Mordecai in the book. The entrance of Haman in the castle court. Who could do this but the blessed Controller of all things? "[God] makes everything work out according to his plan" (Eph. 1:11 NLT).

Even in the most pagan corner of the world. Even in the heart of a hedonist king. Even in the interplay between two men who had decreed the deaths of thousands of Jews, God was at work.

And he is still at work. Do you think the odds are against you? That even God is against you? You've been led to believe that life is a roll of the dice, and you can't remember the last time they rolled in your favor? Does it seem your good deeds go unnoticed? Your integrity unrewarded?

If so, ponder the plight of Haman and the outcome of Mordecai. God flip-flopped their stories. Haman began the day large and in charge, walking into the king's quarters. Mordecai began the day wearing sackcloth and ashes, praying in the shadow of a seven-story gallows that bore his name. Yet from one moment to the next, Haman was humiliated, and Mordecai was given the keys to the city. Haman's death edict became Silly Putty in the hands of God's providence.

The next time you hear someone say, "The devil is in the details," correct them. God is in the details. He works in the small moments. The insignificant becomes significant because he is ever orchestrating the day-to-day details of innumerable lives through a millennia of time to do what he has foreordained to do.

> God is in the details. He works in the small moments.

I know of a mother who can attest to this. Out of respect for her privacy, I won't disclose her name. But I'll tell you her story. She'd decided to end her life. The twists and turns had taken their toll, and she was out of cope. She planned her exit down to the last detail. One of those details was a trip to the bookstore to purchase a children's book for her kids. It would be her parting gift.

She asked the store owner to make a recommendation. He took her to the shelf that contained a book called *Tell Me the Story* by Max Lucado. The mother made the purchase. I know what happened next because she wrote me a letter on the back of the bookstore sack.

This is just a short note to say, "Thank You" for your wonderful book, *Tell Me the Story*. I went to the bookstore today to purchase gifts for several people. For several weeks I have been playing with the idea of killing myself. I have been struggling for years to really "believe and feel" that God is real. I bought this as a "good-bye present" for one of my children. I had no idea what the book said, but it was supposedly Christian and had a pretty cover.

For the next several hours I drove around, crying. I was waiting until my children would be asleep so that I could go home, leave their presents, and disappear forever.

God led me on a little detour, though. My car ran out of oil, and the engine started making that "clicking" sound. I tried to find an open Express Oil or something, but everything was closed. I was frustrated because I needed my car to stay in one piece long enough for me to go home and then go back to some nearby railroad tracks.

I pulled into a nearby parking lot and was sorting through the presents and writing little notes of encouragement on each. For some reason I decided to "waste time" by reading *Tell Me the Story*. I was really touched. . . . I felt as if I was really able to "know" Jesus in a different way. Instead of killing myself tonight, I'm going to go home and keep rereading the book. I want a relationship with God. . . . I'm going to turn my car around, mail this letter and go home and read a story to my kids.

A king can't sleep.

A despondent mom buys a book.

And a Jewish doctor shares his Christian faith with Aleksandr in a Russian prison.

The story of Aleksandr began in 1918. The Russia into which he was born was entering the siege of communism that would starve the populace and destroy its dissidents. Aleksandr, brilliant and precocious, knew from the age of nine he wanted to be a writer. Privy to a library of classics in the home of his aunt, he read giants of Russian literature, including Dostoyevsky and Tolstoy.

Though exposed to the Orthodox faith of his aunt Irina, by early adulthood he was a disciple of Marx and Lenin and avidly read their writings. He was awarded a Stalin scholarship at the university and was on the path to a brilliant literary or academic career. But then, World War II.

Moscow came under siege, and Aleksandr was drafted into a military unit responsible for transportation that used horses. He was ridiculed for his academic achievement and educated language. A soldier's life was no life for him.

But compared to what was to come, it was a honeymoon. Falsely accused of engaging with a spy, he was arrested on February 9, 1945. Thinking it was all a mistake, he was convinced that he would be released in short order. He was wrong. He had been sucked into the hideous undertow of Soviet totalitarianism. Over the next eight years he landed in a succession of prisons, some better than others, but all foreboding. Little by little his faith in the regime diminished. But what would replace it?

Incrementally the faith of his childhood began to reemerge. He met Christian intellectuals, also prisoners, who contributed to his growing conviction. But the decisive stone in the archway was set into place in January 1952 when a large, painful lump appeared in Aleksandr's groin. It was diagnosed as cancerous. As he was recovering from an operation, he received a visit from a Jewish doctor who had just recently become a Christian.[3]

Aleksandr would later describe it this way:

> Fervently he tells me the long story of his conversion from Judaism to Christianity. . . . I am astonished at the conviction of the new convert, at the ardor of his words. . . .
>
> I cannot see his face. Through the window come only the scattered reflections of the lights of the perimeter outside. And the door from the corridor gleams in a yellow electrical glow. But there is such mystical knowledge in his voice that I shudder.[4]

Turns out, this was the last conversation of the doctor's life. Accused of being a stool pigeon, he was bludgeoned to death the next day. Aleksandr never forgot the conversation.

He soon followed in the steps of the doctor, following the steps of the Messiah. His passion for Christ, love for writing, and devotion to freedom resulted in books that many consider to be some of the greatest achievements in literature. I introduced him by his first name. You would recognize Aleksandr by his last name—Solzhenitsyn.

When the world seems off

the rails, hold fast to this truth:

Butterfly wings don't determine

the course of history. God does.

In his classic *The Gulag Archipelago*, he described his conversion.

> And now with measuring cup returned to me,
>
> Scooping up the living water,
>
> God of the Universe! I believe again!
>
> Though I renounced You, You were with me![5]

Some attribute the collapse of Eastern communism, in part, to his writings. Who would have ever imagined that deep in a prison built on atheism a heart would turn to Christ and would touch the world?

Yet another divine reversal.

Yours is coming. Assume that God is at work. Move forward as if God is moving forward in your life. Give no quarter to the voices of doubt and fear. Don't cower to the struggle.

You can't see God's hand? Can't make sense of his ways? That's okay. Obey what you know to do, and be patient for what you don't. "Those who wait on the LORD shall renew their strength" (Isa. 40:31 NKJV).

When the world seems off the rails, hold fast to this truth: Butterfly wings don't determine the course of history. God does. He did in the days of Esther. He still does today.

Chapter Eight

THE WICKED
WILL NOT WIN

A 1962 episode of *The Twilight Zone* tells the story of a vain, harsh man. He bunkers in his apartment, imprisoned by his belief in a big conspiracy theory. He, and only he, perceives the world for what it is: a planet inhabited by people who deserve to die.

The episode begins, as each does, with an introduction by the show's creator and narrator, Rod Serling. He introduces the self-absorbed character. "That's Oliver Crangle, a dealer in petulance and poison." He proceeds to talk about Crangle's "metamorphosis of a twisted fanatic, poisoned by the gangrene of prejudice, to the status of avenging angel, upright and omniscient, dedicated and fearsome."

Crangle is a man of no empathy. He rages against people he has never met. He demands that their employers fire them. He calls on law enforcement to arrest them. Crangle ascends a judicial bench of self-righteousness and proclaims a guilty sentence on everyone else.

He concocts a plan to purge the world of unsavory folk. He informs the FBI that at 4:00 p.m. all the world's despicable and evil people will be easy to identify and imprison. Crangle will shrink them to a height of two feet.

Justice will finally be served. Evildoers will be disclosed, and he will be seen for the hero he is. As the fateful hour draws near, Crangle can hardly contain himself with excitement. Out of his mind with anticipation, he hurries to his window at 4:00 p.m. to celebrate the day of reckoning. But, alas, he is too small to look out the glass. He, Crangle, has been shrunk. He stands two feet tall.[1]

Do you know a Mr. Crangle? Have you crossed trails with small-minded, self-centered, despicable oppressors who view the world from a perch of arrogance? They abuse. They bully. They scorn. They enslave. They even seek to exterminate.

Haman was a Crangle. The villain of Esther's story lived inside a one-person world. Everyone else existed to bow down to him. When one of them didn't, Haman declared his fate and the fate of his people: death. Yet Haman's swagger was short-lived. His reign of terror came to an end in the dining hall of Xerxes.

> So the king and Haman went to Queen Esther's banquet, and as they were drinking wine on the second day, the king again asked, "Queen Esther, what is your petition? It will be given you. What is your request? Even up to half the kingdom, it will be granted." (Est. 7:1–2)

This was feast number two. Much has happened since feast number one. Haman plotted the death of Mordecai. Xerxes honored the dedication of Mordecai. Haman, who demanded to be worshiped, was humiliated. Mordecai, who refused to worship Haman, was celebrated. Haman was so angry and distraught he almost missed the party.

Banquet number two was every bit as elaborate as banquet number one. The wine was abundant. There was food aplenty. The festivity helped Haman forget his miserable day. He was just about to pour himself another goblet of wine when the king asked the queen what she desired. He'd asked this question before. Esther had deferred. But now the time was right. Her heart rate must have registered in the triple digits as she spoke.

If I have found favor with you, Your Majesty, and if it pleases you, grant me my life—this is my petition. And spare my people—this is my request. For I and my people have been sold to be destroyed, killed and annihilated. If we had merely been sold as male and female slaves, I would have kept quiet, because no such distress would justify disturbing the king. (vv. 3–4)

The key words are the small words: "*I . . . me . . . my . . . I* and *my* people . . . to be destroyed . . . killed . . . if *we* had merely been sold as . . . slaves . . .*"

Esther the Persian queen revealed that she was Esther the Jew. She linked her fate to the fate of her people. Silence fell on the room like a curtain. The king's head was surely spinning. He struggled to connect the dots. *Someone is plotting to kill the Jews? And you are a Jew? Someone is plotting to kill my queen?*

"Who is he, and where is he? Who has done such a thing?"

Esther said, "Our enemy and foe is this wicked Haman!"

Then Haman was filled with terror before the king and queen.

(vv. 5–6 NCV)

Haman, all two feet of him, began to tremble. He had no recourse. Both his jaw and goblet dropped.

Xerxes stormed out of the room. Livid. Fuming. Seething with rage. He was angry at Haman for playing him the fool, angry at himself for being one.

The blood drained from Haman's face. Unless he acted quickly, it would soon drain from his body. He threw himself on the mercy of Esther. Literally. He fell onto her couch. Xerxes reentered the room and saw Haman groping toward the queen. Haman, who wanted to kill a Jew for not falling down in his presence, was caught falling down before a Jew. The ironies continue.

The guards hooded Haman's head and took him into custody (v. 8). One of the king's officials looked out the window at the seventy-five-foot gallows. "If I might make a suggestion, your majesty . . ." Xerxes gave the nod and Haman got the point.

While there is more to be resolved in the story of Esther (namely, an irreversible edict from the king to kill the Jews), we need to highlight a significant theme in this book.

Our God is a just God.

Nothing escapes him. No one escapes him. The wicked will not win.

Belshazzar learned this truth firsthand. He became king of Babylon in 539 BC, some fifty-three years before the reign of Xerxes.

In a fateful feast Belshazzar invited one thousand of his gentry to join him in a celebration. His banquet hall was reportedly 1,650 feet wide and a mile long. "Some 4,500 pillars in the form of giant elephants were part of the walls."[2] There was music, feasting, and, you guessed it, much wine.

> While Belshazzar was drinking his wine, he gave orders to bring in the gold and silver goblets that Nebuchadnezzar his father had taken from the temple in Jerusalem, so that the king and his nobles, his wives and his concubines might drink from them. So they brought in the gold goblets that had been taken from the temple of God in Jerusalem, and the king and his nobles, his wives and his concubines drank from them. As they drank the wine, they praised the gods of gold and silver, of bronze, iron, wood and stone. (Dan. 5:2–4)

When Nebuchadnezzar's armies sacked the temple and burned it to the ground some fifty years earlier, they took everything of value. This included the menorah, the altar of incense, the table of holy bread, bowls and pitchers. These utensils stayed untouched in storage

Our God is a just God.

Nothing escapes him.

No one escapes him.

The wicked will not win.

for half a century until Belshazzar threw this party. The king commanded that the temple implements be used as wine goblets.

Why? Were they running low on glasses? Was the dishwasher broken? Was the kitchen team on strike? No, there was only one reason. The king wanted to blaspheme the God of Israel. Belshazzar made a mockery of Jehovah. He used holy utensils in a drunken, pagan celebration. His irreverence did not go unnoticed. Out of the sleeve of the night a mysterious hand came into view.

> Suddenly the fingers of a human hand appeared and wrote on the plaster of the wall, near the lampstand in the royal palace. The king watched the hand as it wrote. His face turned pale and he was so frightened that his legs became weak and his knees were knocking. (Dan. 5:5–6)

Can you envision the moment? A hand, detached from a body, appeared out of thin air. It hovered in the glow of a lampstand. The finger of the hand carved a message into the plaster of the wall. The room became as quiet as sleep. Belshazzar trembled so much he collapsed. His sneer became a frown. His boast became a whimper. He heard nothing but the pounding of his own heart.

The people could not decipher the meaning. The king called for his astrologers and diviners to be brought in. "Interpret the message," he said, "and you will be rich and powerful!" (v. 7). But they were clueless.

His queen heard the commotion and entered the banquet hall. When she saw the king, she said, "Don't be alarmed! Don't look so pale! There is a man in your kingdom who has the spirit of the holy gods in him. . . . Call for Daniel, and he will tell you what the writing means" (vv. 10–12).

Daniel was summoned. By this point his hair was silver. His back was slightly stooped from the years. But his mind and faith were keen and as honed as steel. Belshazzar offered him money and power. Daniel told the king to keep them both. He then reminded Belshazzar how God had punished Belshazzar's father with a season of insanity. The son should have been paying attention. But he wasn't.

> "But you, Belshazzar, his son, have not humbled yourself, though you knew all this. Instead, you have set yourself up against the Lord of heaven. . . . Therefore he sent the hand that wrote the inscription.
>
> "This is the inscription that was written:
>
> MENE, MENE, TEKEL, PARSIN
>
> "Here is what these words mean:
>
> *Mene*: God has numbered the days of your reign and brought it to an end.
>
> *Tekel*: You have been weighed on the scales and found wanting.
>
> *Peres*: Your kingdom is divided and given to the Medes and Persians."
>
> . . . That very night Belshazzar, king of the Babylonians, was slain, and Darius the Mede took over the kingdom, at the age of sixty-two. (vv. 22–28; 29–31)

At the precise moment Daniel was explaining the prophecy, the Medo-Persian armies were creeping through the underground aqueducts, preparing to take the city. Belshazzar never saw the attack coming. The takeover was fast and total. The mighty nation of Babylon collapsed, Belshazzar was killed, and we are left with a sobering reminder: our God is a just God.

"Behold therefore the goodness and severity of God" (Rom. 11:22 KJV). Goodness *and* severity. We can't take one and disregard the other. God is good. Yet he is also severe.

We seldom discuss this attribute of our Father. God's kindness? Often mentioned. His forgiveness? The theme of many sermons. Hymns that herald his mercy? Too many to count. But songs that acknowledge his wrath, that look toward the day of retribution? Not so many.

The Bible, on the other hand, is not shy on the subject. Out of curiosity I compared the number of Scripture references on the two topics. God's wrath is mentioned more than 150 times; his mercy, 32 times.[3]

> It is right to declare God's goodness. But it is a mistake to dismiss God's justice.

To be sure, it is right to declare God's goodness. But it is a mistake to dismiss God's justice. He is gracious to those who trust him, but he is serious about punishing those who dismiss him.

For some of you this is a word of caution. Don't think for a moment that God turns a blind eye to acts of rebellion and deeds of malice. "He will judge everyone according to what they have done" (Rom. 2:6 NLT). Today's adultery is tomorrow's divorce. Today's indulgence is tomorrow's addiction. Today's dishonesty is tomorrow's dismissal. Most supremely, dismiss God in this life, and he will dismiss you in the next.

For others this can be a word of comfort. Hamans worm their way into our worlds, and when they do, our calendars flip to January, and cold winds begin to blow. We wonder, *Does God know what this Haman is doing? Does God care about my suffering? Will Haman ever meet justice?*

Or to borrow the words of the psalmist: "O Lord, how long will you look on?" (Ps. 35:17 GW). Or the question of Jeremiah: "Why does the way of the wicked prosper?" (Jer. 12:1). Do evildoers get a free pass? Do oppressors walk free? Do Hamans and Hitlers, lynch mobs, and vigilantes get away with murder?

The Bible's answer is a resounding *no*! God "has set a day when he will judge the world" (Acts 17:31). The aggressor who took advantage of you? God knows. The government official who embezzled money from the poor? God knows. The bigot who raged, the misogynist who raped, the bully who belittled? God knows.

And what about the innocent? How many millions of people have spent their lives in workhouses and labor camps or as victims of sex trafficking? God knows about them all. "God is a just judge, and God is angry with the wicked every day" (Ps. 7:11 NKJV).

God's righteous indignation is on high boil, and his call to you and me is straightforward: get involved! "Whoever shuts their ears to the cry of the poor will also cry out and not be answered" (Prov. 21:13).

> When we cry out, "God, do something!" he says, "I did. I created you."

When we cry out, "God, do something!" he says, "I did. I created you."

The prophet Isaiah lived at a time when injustice and immorality were pervasive. "Truth is nowhere to be found, and whoever shuns evil becomes a prey. The LORD looked and was displeased that there was no justice. He saw that there was no one, he was appalled that there was no one to intervene" (Isa. 59:15–16).

It wasn't enough for God's people to long for justice. God called them to be creators of justice.

> "This is the kind of fast day I'm after:
>   to break the chains of injustice,
>   get rid of exploitation in the workplace,
>   free the oppressed,
>   cancel debts.
> What I'm interested in seeing you do is:
>   sharing your food with the hungry,
>   inviting the homeless poor into your homes,
>   putting clothes on the shivering ill-clad,
>   being available to your own families.

Do this and the lights will turn on,
   and your lives will turn around at once.
Your righteousness will pave your way.
   The GOD of glory will secure your passage.
Then when you pray, GOD will answer.
   You'll call out for help and I'll say, "Here I am."

(ISA. 58:6–8 THE MESSAGE)

Justice happens to the degree that we align ourselves with God's hand of fairness. When you do, when you teach a disabled child to walk or read, when you care for the elderly whose sight is dim or memory is fading, when you rally support for the marginalized or oppressed, you accomplish something that will continue into the world to come. It's a wonderful thing to restore art, antique cars, or dilapidated houses. But it is a holy thing to restore human dignity. That is what Charles Mulli is doing.

He grew up as the oldest of ten children in a small village in Machakos County, Kenya. His father was violent. His upbringing was poor. When he was six, Mulli's family abandoned him. They left him with an aunt. He survived by begging from house to house, village to village. Bitter from the abandonment and abuse by his father, he contemplated taking his own life. Redemption came in the form of an invitation to visit a church. At the age of eighteen Mulli found Jesus and, in doing so, found energy to improve his lot.

He walked the seventy-kilometer journey to Nairobi and knocked on doors, looking for work. He was hired to do housework in a wealthy businessman's home. Invigorated by the fresh start, Mulli rose into management at the man's company. He eventually began his own enterprise, Mullyways, providing transportation between the capital and local villages. Success followed him everywhere. He expanded into oil, gas, and real estate and eventually purchased fifty acres of land in the Ndalani region for future retirement.

It's a wonderful thing to
restore art, antique cars,
or dilapidated houses.
But it is a holy thing to
restore human dignity.

His story took a turn one day on a business trip. A group of street children asked to watch his car in exchange for money. He declined, only to return and discover that his car was gone. On the bus ride home he began to struggle, not with anger at the thieves, but with disappointment in himself. He had forgotten his own beginnings. He'd ignored the street children. After all, they were just like him!

For three years he wrestled with his conscience. Finally in November 1989 at the age of forty, he left his companies behind to rescue street children. He heard the voice of God: "You will never let my children suffer. You have to rescue them and become the father to the fatherless." Though he already had eight children, he and his wife took in three more kids from the street. Six years later they were caring for three hundred. As of the writing of this book, the six campuses of his ministry house are reaching roughly thirty-five hundred children, and some twenty-three thousand children have been served.

"I went to the street with one purpose: to rescue children," explained Mulli. "Every child needs food, love, accommodation, education, protection, [a] good and bright future. Who then will reach to them with that love of Christ? I was one of them, one who is lost."[4]

Mulli became a part of the solution.

When we do the same, when we join hands with God, justice finds oxygen, and oppression hides in the corner.

To be clear, the day is coming when God will forever balance the scales of justice. The glory of the new kingdom will be hallmarked by prosperity and justice. The next life will have no need for rescue missions, welfare programs, homeless shelters, or relief agencies. God promised:

> No more building a house
> > that some outsider takes over,
> No more planting fields
> > that some enemy confiscates,

For my people will be as long-lived as trees,

    my chosen ones will have satisfaction in their work.

They won't work and have nothing come of it,

    they won't have children snatched out from under them.

For they themselves are plantings blessed by GOD,

    with their children and grandchildren likewise GOD-blessed.

                                  (ISA. 65:22–23 THE MESSAGE)

Until then let's partner with him in the pursuit of what is right. Relief will come, and we can be a part of it. Stand up for the downtrodden. Take up the cause of the poor. Remember the plight of the forgotten, and in doing so enjoy God's approval.

It comes down to each one of us choosing to silence the Hamans of the world through kindness and love. When you speak for the forgotten and stand up for the downtrodden, justice has a chance, and Satan has a fit. He can't even see out the window. After all, he's only two feet tall.

Chapter Nine

THE GOD OF GREAT TURNAROUNDS

Dalia is a Christian missionary to the Muslims in her native country. She lives where Christians are not welcome. For that reason I won't tell you her real name or the name of her homeland. But her story? It is worth hearing.

She plants seed on rocky soil. After decades of service she's seen only a handful of converts. One is a woman Dalia met a decade ago. We will call her Ayesha. Both were single at the time. Dalia, a widow. Ayesha had never married. They met in a sewing class. Over the months the two became friends. And in the cloak of secrecy, Ayesha became friends with Jesus Christ.

She progressed in her faith and was deepening her spiritual roots when she fell in love. Her suitor was not a believer. He did not know she was. She feared to tell him. In fact, as Ayesha told Dalia, her country had so few male Christians that if she waited to marry one, she might never have a family. Against Dalia's advice Ayesha accepted the man's marriage proposal.

She pledged to read her Bible every day. "I will hide it where he cannot find it," she promised. And so she did. She married her Muslim husband and hid her Christian Bible.

A few months after the wedding Dalia had a dream. In it God told her to talk to Ayesha's husband about Jesus. She awoke in a cold sweat. She could not do this! For one thing, in her patriarchal culture women do not initiate conversations with men, especially married men. And in her Muslim world Christians live in fear of persecution. She revealed her faith at risk of death.

Still, God had spoken. Dalia shared the dream with Ayesha. And, like Esther, they devised a plan.

Dalia invited the couple over for a dinner. During the meal she invited them to watch a film with her, an American-made movie about Jesus. Much to the relief of the two women, the husband thought the idea was harmless. They set a date to watch the movie in his house. For days Dalia and Ayesha prayed.

When the evening finally arrived, Dalia gathered herself and set out for their home. They ate and then began watching the *Jesus* film. As one of the most effective evangelism tools in history, it has been translated into more than sixteen hundred spoken languages all over the world, including the dialect spoken by Dalia and her friends.

During the movie Dalia kept glancing toward Ayesha's husband, wondering what he was thinking. He showed no response. At its conclusion the trio sat in silence. After a long pause he stood and walked into the adjacent room. The women looked at each other, unsure what to do. Was he angry? Was he leaving? They did not know. Presently he returned, holding the Bible that Ayesha had hidden.

"I know you have been reading this book," he said.

They gasped. Then to their surprise he added, "So have I. I've been reading about this Jesus. I'd like to know more about him."

Dalia's eyes filled with tears. Ayesha's heart filled with hope. In time the husband became a Christian. He and his wife are raising their children to know Jesus.[1]

From one moment to the next, the story of Ayesha's home took a turn. And we are reminded yet again that no condition is too dark, no situation is too difficult, no problem is so severe that God can't intervene, overturn, and reverse the course of events. Isn't this the promise of the story of Esther?

Esther chapter 9 opens with these words:

On the thirteenth day of the twelfth month, the month of Adar, the edict commanded by the king was to be carried out. On this day the enemies of the Jews had hoped to overpower them, but now *the tables were turned* and the Jews got the upper hand over those who hated them. (v. 1, emphasis mine)

Other translations read:

"The exact opposite happened." (GW)
"The reverse occurred." (ESV)
"Their plan was overturned." (BSB)
"It turned out to the contrary." (NASB)

The versions vary but state the same promise: God is the God of the plot twist.

Every good story has one. Every good movie has a moment that leaves the viewer thinking, *I never saw that coming.* A good writer masters the art of rerouting the arc of the narrative: what the reader thought would happen did not, and what happened, the reader never imagined.

Exactly what did happen in Esther's case? God softened a hard heart.

That same day King Xerxes gave Queen Esther the estate of Haman, the enemy of the Jews. And Mordecai came into the presence of the king, for Esther had told how he was related to her. (8:1)

Remember, this is Xerxes. With a wave of his hand, he could dispense with a queen. With an impression of his ring, he could condemn an entire race. When his thumb went up, people lived. When his thumb went down? No one was betting on a kind reply from the king. Yet a higher king was at work.

> [Xerxes] took off his signet ring, which he had reclaimed from Haman, and presented it to Mordecai. And Esther appointed him over Haman's estate. (v. 2)

The signet ring that once graced the hand of Haman now graced the hand of Mordecai, a gift from the king. The reversals continue to stack up. Yet for all the good that had occurred, something horrific was about to happen.

> Esther again pleaded with the king, falling at his feet and weeping. She begged him to put an end to the evil plan of Haman the Agagite, which he had devised against the Jews. (v. 3)

Esther's people weren't out of the woods. The Jews were still under a sentence of death. The law was irrevocable. Not even Xerxes could undo it. Most modern societies have the freedom to change a law if it is proven unfavorable. Ancient Persia, however, saw the king as divine. An edict of his could not be undone even if he wanted to undo it! (Odd, I know.)

Maybe you are facing something similar. Are you staring at an unscalable wall or impossible challenge?

Then you're going to love what happened next.

Xerxes amended the law. The king told Esther and Mordecai, "Now write another decree in the king's name in behalf of the Jews as seems best to you, and seal it with the king's signet ring—for no document written in the king's name and sealed with his ring can be revoked" (v. 8).

It was a work-around! The king couldn't reverse the law, so he wrote a second one. The law of the Medes and Persians could not be changed. So "the king granted the Jews who were in each and every city the right to assemble and to defend their lives" (v. 11 NASB).

This decree was sent out in the third month (v. 9), leaving the Jews nine months to prepare. On the very day the Jews were destined to die, they dealt a blow to the anti-Semitic empire, killing seventy-five thousand men in the king's provinces. Haman's terror was defanged, his family was destroyed, and Mordecai was positioned as the new prime minister of Persia.

It was only pages ago that Haman convinced the world's most powerful man to declare open season on all the Jews and their possessions. The outlook at the end of chapter 3 could not have been bleaker.

Haman was hard-hearted and pompous.

Xerxes was out of touch and oblivious.

All the sons and daughters of Abraham had a price on their heads. Bigotry. Hatred. Xenophobia. Greed. Those forces were going to win the day. At least so it seemed. But then came the *peripety parade*.

If you need a synonym for *plot twist*, try *peripety*. It's a literary device that describes a redirected story line. It's that moment in the book that causes you to stay up past your bedtime because you can't believe what just happened. In the case of Esther:

Mordecai found a spine and refused to bow.

Esther's three-day fast resulted in a surge of courage.

Esther told the king what Haman intended to do. Haman went from second-in-command to shish kebab on a stake. Mordecai went from sackcloth to the king's robes. God's people went from Esther 4:3 to Esther 8:16.

In Esther 4:3: "There was great mourning among the Jews, with fasting, weeping and wailing. Many lay in sackcloth and ashes."

But by the time we reach chapter 8: "For the Jews it was a time of happiness and joy, gladness and honor" (v. 16).

Do you find yourself in the fourth chapter of the Esther story?

Are your days marked by mourning, fasting, weeping, and lamenting? Does the promise of a reversal seem too distant, too remote?

Maybe an illness has taken its toll. Sorrow has taken your joy. Maybe you live under the shadow of a Haman. You report to a self-centered creep. Your elected officials are out of touch with reality. You are married to a spouse who isn't the same spouse you married. Your skin color isn't the accepted color of your culture.

The struggles of life have pilfered the life out of your life, and you don't know where to turn. You've been disappointed so many times. And you are so very, very tired.

If that is you, I'm sorry. I truly am. It stinks, I know. But I urge you—with every ounce of energy I can muster, I urge you—don't give in to despair. The anaconda of hopelessness will squeeze the life out of you. You can't give up. You just can't. There is too much at stake.

Your Bible invites you to believe in a coming peripety.

- Abraham and Sarah were old and barren one day and then saucer-eyed and pregnant the next. Peripety.
- Joseph went to sleep one night as an Egyptian prisoner. He went to sleep the next night as the Egyptian prime minister. Peripety.
- The Red Sea was uncrossable one minute and a pathway the next. Peripety.
- Joshua marched seven times around the city of Jericho. After the sixth circle the walls were standing. After the seventh they were rubble. Peripety.
- Goliath defied Israel for forty days. But then David loaded a peripety in his sling and let it fly. Down went the giant.
- The 450 prophets of Baal mocked Jehovah, but then Elijah prayed, and a fire-filled peripety fell from heaven.
- The lions wanted to eat Daniel one moment, but they couldn't open their mouths the next. Their jaws were wired shut with divine peripety.

Do you sense the rhythm? In God's hands no script is predictable, no story line is inevitable, no outcome is certain. He is ever a turn of the page from a turn-on-a-dime turnaround. For heaven's sake look in the Bethlehem barn. Who saw this coming? Or better asked, who saw *him* coming? God sleeping in a feed trough, still moist from Mary's womb. He held the universe in one moment and squeezed Mary's pinkie the next.

He is the God of grand reversals.

The greatest reversal occurred in a cemetery outside of Jerusalem. Jesus the Christ was Jesus the corpse. No pulse. No breath. No hope. Wrapped tighter than an Egyptian mummy and three days dead in a borrowed tomb. His enemies raised a toast to a dead Messiah.

And his followers? They weren't scattered in the provinces of Persia, but they were hiding in the bare cupboards and corners of Jerusalem for fear of a cross that bore their names. Their world was broken. Their hearts were broken.

They'd left everything to follow Jesus. The fishermen left nets. The tax collectors left jobs. They left it all. And now it seemed Jesus had returned the favor. He left them. Thanks to three nails and a cross, the light of the world had gone dark . . . or so it seemed. The Savior of humanity couldn't save himself . . . or so it seemed. Heaven's hope was a hoax. The redeemer was a joke. Jesus, the Son of God, had been done in by the devil, the Haman of hell . . . or so it seemed.

And just when all joy was lost, peripety! His heart began to beat. Eyelids popped open. Pierced hands lifted, and Jesus stood up and placed his heel squarely on the head of Satan.

And when he did:

"The tables were turned."

"The exact opposite happened."

"The reverse occurred."

"Their plan was overturned."

"It turned out to the contrary."

God is ever a turn

of the page from

a turn-on-a-dime

turnaround.

No matter how you write it, the Easter morning announcement is the same: "[Christ] isn't here! He is risen from the dead, just as he said would happen. Come, see where his body was lying" (Matt. 28:6 NLT). The God of great turnarounds performed his greatest work.

Who's to say he doesn't have a reversal in your future? Don't let the middle of the story confuse you. Don't be thrown off by the prosperity of the wicked or the seeming success of the Hamans of the world. Instead, set your eyes on the author of your salvation.

No individual, institution, organization, society, or country is beyond the influence of God. I repeat, no one is beyond his sovereign hand. "The Lord directs the king's thoughts. He turns them wherever he wants to" (Prov. 21:1 TLB).

For witness to this truth I'd like to call someone to the stand: Vinh Chung. His dark eyes sparkle. His cheekbones lift with his ever-present smile. His sizable frame served him well in Arkansas, where he played high school football, and in Australia, where he played rugby. His résumé impresses the most impressive. He is a dermatologist with a degree from Harvard and the recipient of numerous awards. Yet his statement matters, not because of where he is today, but because of where he was at the age of three.

When I was three and a half years old, my family was forced to leave Vietnam and flee to a place we had never heard of, somewhere in the heartland of America, called Arkansas.

I am a refugee.

My family went to sleep in one world and woke up in another.... We arrived in this country with nothing but the clothes on our backs and unable to speak a single word of English; my family now holds twenty-one university degrees, including five master's and five doctorates from institutions such as Harvard, Yale, Georgetown, Stanford, George Mason, Michigan, and Arkansas.

But in July 1979, my family lay half-dead from dehydration in a derelict fishing boat jammed with ninety-three refugees lost in the middle of the South China Sea.

How we got from there to here is quite a story.[2]

Vinh Chung was born in South Vietnam just eight months after it fell to the communists in 1975. His family was wealthy, controlling a rice-milling empire worth millions of dollars. But within months of the communist takeover, they lost everything. Their business was confiscated, and they were evicted from their own home.

Knowing that their children would have no future under the new government, the Chungs decided to flee the country. In 1979 they joined the legendary boat people and sailed into the South China Sea, despite knowing that an estimated two hundred thousand Vietnamese had already perished as a result of brutal pirates and violent waters.

> Who's to say God doesn't have a reversal in your future?

They boarded a rickety vessel with some three hundred other fugitives. Living conditions were abhorrent. Food was rationed. Drinking water was scarce. Sleep was rare. Nausea was common. Marauding Thai pirates raided the boat and took their meager possessions.

The Chungs finally made it to a Malaysian beach. The refugee camp refused them. Malaysian military beat the men and marched the family for days across the hot sands. Chung's mother nearly died from a miscarriage and loss of blood. When a second refugee camp turned them away, the Malaysian authorities loaded the Vietnamese on small fishing boats, tugged them out to sea, and cut them loose.

Ninety-three people pressed skin against skin beneath the boiling sun. They had one gallon of water. Capfuls of the precious liquid were given, just to the children. The boat had no motor or sail. The people had no oars. The ever-undulating waters left them seasick. The heat left them parched. The empty horizon offered no hope.

After five days at sea Mr. Chung did something his family had never seen him do. He looked into the dehydrated and hungry faces, picked himself up from his cross-legged position, knelt in the center of the boat, and prayed. *I know there is a Creator God. I know you created us and don't want us to die like this. So, if you're listening, please send rain.*

Within moments the sky darkened and rain fell. No lightning. No thunder. Just relief. There was a reprieve from the heat. But the families were still adrift. On day number six the heat and fear returned.

They had no way of knowing, but help was on the way.

I never met Stan Mooneyham. But I am well acquainted with his legacy. He served as president of World Vision from 1969 to 1982. World Vision is one of the largest relief agencies in the world. To hear the old-timers talk about Stan, he was unstoppable. A story of forgotten or abused people sent him into a flurry of activity. When he heard about the boat people, he went right to work.

World Vision chartered a World War II landing ship, loaded it with food, water, diesel fuel, and medical supplies and set sail out of the Singapore harbor. By the time they rescued the boat that carried the Chung family, Operation Seasweep had already saved hundreds of refugees in the South China Sea.

According to Mooneyham the boat that carried the Chung family was no more than a day away from falling apart. He loaded the exiles onto the ship and began treatment. The four-day trip to Singapore consisted of rest, recovery, and Bible studies. Mr. Chung was not a religious man. So why did he attend the church service? He wanted to know why these people rescued them while the rest of the world ignored them.

The answer from Mooneyham? Jesus. Mooneyham described Christ's love for the unloved, his compassion and kindness. Vinh Chung would later write: "[My father] suddenly recognized that all the seemingly random events of his life had a purpose. . . . At that moment my father felt his entire past had been dropped into the South

China Sea—he was free; he was forgiven. Now he knew the Creator God had a name and a face, and my father knew he would never be the same again."[3]

There is much more to the odyssey of this family. Perhaps, however, these paragraphs are adequate to demonstrate my belief that the God of Esther and Mordecai is alive and well. He still hears the prayers of exiles, and he still uses the faithful to reach them.

Are you in need of rescue?

Are you available to rescue someone else?

Either way, keep praying. Keep trusting. Your story is not finished. For all you know you may be a day away from a game-changing peripety. Tonight could be the night that Xerxes won't sleep and a chain of events will be set in motion that will forever change your life. Reversals happen.

But you have to stay in the game. Mordecai did. Esther did. Dalia and Ayesha did. The Chungs did. Mooneyham did. All could have taken a different path. They chose the path of faith. Because they did, each of their stories took a turn for the better.

So will yours, my friend. So will yours.

Chapter Ten

A PURIM PEOPLE

There is a big bug in the middle of Enterprise, Alabama. It sits on a statue of a Greek woman. She has white marble arms that extend high above her head somewhat like the Statue of Liberty. Unlike her more famous counterpart, the Alabama lady does not hold a torch. She holds a bug. Well, strictly speaking, she holds a bowl, and on the bowl is a boll weevil. The insect weighs fifty pounds and is celebrated by a nearby plaque: "In profound appreciation of the Boll Weevil and what it has done as the Herald of Prosperity."

The statue was erected in 1919. The bug was added thirty years later. Who does this? Why make a big deal out of an ugly weevil? Since its arrival from Mexico in 1892, the pest has cost the cotton industry more than $23 billion. The insect does to cotton fields what teenagers do to pizza. Gone in a gobble. By the 1920s boll weevils were having their way with the Alabama crops. They could not and would not be eradicated.

So why honor them with a statue? The answer to that question involves a seed seller by the name of H. M. Sessions. He saw what was happening with the cash crop and knew he needed to act. In 1916 on a trip through Virginia and North Carolina, Sessions saw peanut fields. He came to learn that peanuts were impervious to the boll weevil. So he came home with peanut seeds and sold them to C. W. Baston. Baston planted them and made $8,000 from his new crop. He paid off his debt and still had money left over. Word spread quickly. Farmers jumped on the peanut bus and rode it straight to the bank. By 1919, when the boll weevil scourge was wreaking its worst havoc, Coffee County, Alabama, was the largest producer of peanuts in the nation.[1]

Let's talk about your boll weevils, shall we? Cotton-chewing varmints have swarmed into your world. Unwelcome pests, are they not? Toll-taking scoundrels. How dare they feast on your harvest? Now the barns are empty, and there are questions aplenty. *What do I do? Where do I turn?*

Let me add one more question to your list. Might the bugs actually be a blessing? The boll weevil took much, for sure. But had there been no bug, there would have been no peanut harvest. Or, in your case, no struggle means no strength. No mountain means no mountain peak. No setback means no comeback, and a comeback is yours for the taking. Yes, I'm saying what you think I'm saying: boll weevils make us better.

This is the anthem of the story of Esther.

The Jewish people, once joyful inhabitants of Israel, were scattered like dry leaves in a winter wind. They had no temple. No homeland. No leader. Where is the Joshua of the day? The David or Elijah? Nowhere to be found. The Jews were leaderless minnows in the ocean that was Persia.

And Persia? Its king was a louse. His chief of staff was a thug. The two Jews of prominence, Mordecai and Esther, had chosen to keep their nationality a secret.

It wasn't the best of times for God's covenant people. Boll weevils everywhere.

But then Mordecai and Esther planted some peanuts. He took a stand. She took a risk. Haman died on his own gallows. The Jews took up arms and defeated the Persians. The day of their scheduled defeat became the day of certain victory. "[Xerxes] issued a decree causing Haman's plot to boomerang, and he and his sons were hanged on the gallows" (Est. 9:25 TLB). And "Mordecai the Jew was second in rank to King Xerxes, preeminent among the Jews, and held in high esteem by his many fellow Jews, because he worked for the good of his people and spoke up for the welfare of all the Jews" (10:3).

V-day celebrations erupted in all corners. A new chapter was written in the history of the Jewish people. They realized they could embrace their identity, even in exile, and trust the hidden hand of God. There was no need to hide their nationality. A person of faith could be a person of influence. Mordecai, the man at the gate, became Mordecai, the Jew in the court. Esther, the quiet queen, became Esther, the Jewish heroine. The entire nation experienced a "refounding of the Jewish people on an entirely different basis."[2] It was a revival of sorts, a renewal.

To ensure that the Jews would remember this moment, Mordecai and Esther commissioned an annual commemoration.

> Mordecai recorded these events, and he sent letters to all the Jews throughout the provinces of King Xerxes, near and far, to have them celebrate annually the fourteenth and fifteenth days of the month of Adar as the time when the Jews got relief from their enemies, and as the month when their sorrow was turned into joy and their mourning into a day of celebration. He wrote them to observe the days as days of feasting and joy and giving presents of food to one another and gifts to the poor. (9:20–22)

The book of Esther does not end with victory in battle. It ends with a call to remember. Just as Christians read the story of the birth of Christ at Christmas, the Jews read the story of Esther during the feast of Purim. The holiday is to be commemorated after the scheduled day of execution, a reminder that the day has come and gone, and the Jews are still standing.

Purim holidays are rowdy affairs, a bit like a masquerade party.

There is an abundance of food, drink, and costumes. As the story is read, the audience reacts. Haman's name prompts loud boos, hisses, and shouts. The idea is to muffle the very sound of his appearance.

"In a controversial passage of the Talmud, Jews are instructed to drink wine [on Purim] until they can't tell the difference between the phrases 'Cursed is Haman' and 'Blessed is Mordecai.'"[3] This practice is not recommended for the church.

A more reasonable tradition would be the baking of the haman-taschen, a three-cornered, jelly-filled pastry. The hidden jelly recalls the hiddenness of God.[4]

I like that tradition. Jelly is sweet, tasty, and when hidden in a doughnut, a surprise to discover. I like the idea that God's presence, scrumptious and unseen, is baked into the story of redemption. And I appreciate the value of a two-day celebration in which people of faith revisit the day and way their God prevailed.

We tend to forget.

We tend to forget that God is for us, not against us. That God is near us, not away from us. That God is busy, not sleepy. We tend to forget that God can make beauty out of ashes, joy out of mourning, an army out of a valley of dry bones, and rejoicing out of sorrow. We need memorials that jog our memory.

One of the most profound observances of Purim included no wine or pastries. There was none to be had. The celebrants were barely alive. The congregation consisted of eighty men crammed into a half-buried hut. Their bodies were racked by typhus and dysentery. Their clothing hung like rags from their frail bodies. They subsisted on a daily portion of bread and soup. They had no hope, no solution. They were prisoners of Auschwitz.

J. J. Cohen was among them. He was a teenager living in a Polish ghetto when he was taken to a death camp. He survived the Holocaust and later remembered the day the prisoners remembered Purim. They took a fragment of potato and a small piece of bread and passed them from person to person in order to fulfill the tradition of giving gifts of food to one another. It fell to young Cohen to relate the story of Esther.

> When I read aloud about Haman's downfall . . . the spark of hope deep inside every Jew's heart ignited into a flaming torch. . . . When I finished, everyone cheered. For a brief instant, the dreadful reality of the death camp had been forgotten, all the hunger and suffering had receded. Having exerted all my remaining energy in my reading of the [story], I sat breathless, but with my spirit soaring. . . . And like a river overflowing its banks, the festive atmosphere and the vision of redemption burst out of the broken hearts of the camp inmates.[5]

I try to envision those men, those skeletal men. I incline an ear into this moment to hear their cheer, anemic yet triumphant. And I wonder, *What kind of story can do this? What sort of narrative has the power to lift the spirits of dead men walking?*

Do we not need such a story today?

We have one.

Satan's scheme to kill the Son of God was defeated on the cross he designed for Christ. Don't you know the devil wanted to puke when he realized that the cross, a tool of death, had become an instrument for life? Had Satan known that the death of the Messiah would mean death for him and life for us, he never would have crucified Jesus.

He never saw it coming.

So that we would never forget this moment, Jesus gave us our own Purim celebration. On the eve of his crucifixion,

> Jesus took some bread, gave thanks, broke it, and gave it to the apostles, saying, "This is my body, which I am giving for you. Do this to remember me." In the same way, after supper, Jesus took

the cup and said, "This cup is the new agreement that God makes with his people. This new agreement begins with my blood which is poured out for you." (Luke 22:19–20 NCV)

Those words are precious to the Christian. But they must have been curious to the apostles. A broken body? Spilled blood? Can good come from this?

And you. Your broken world. Your leaky faith. Your fragile dreams. Can good come from this?

Esther says, "Yes."

Easter says, "Yes."

Purim says, "Yes."

Communion says, "Yes."

This is the promise of God.

It just falls to us to receive it. Receive the cup. Receive the bread. Receive the pastry with its hidden sweetness.

Don't be done in by bad news. Don't fall victim to the voices of panic and chaos. Don't drink the Kool-Aid. You have a good God, who has a good plan, and that plan is revealed in his good book. Today's confusion and crisis will be tomorrow's conquest.

My friend Linda accepted his invitation. Her life has been ravaged by a Hurricane Katrina of troubles. She was raised in a loveless home in western Pennsylvania. Her mother sent her out each morning with a raw potato, a pack of matches, and the reminder: "Come home by dark." Linda and her older sister Nancy would play unattended all day in the woods nearby, make a fire to cook their potatoes for lunch, swim in the creek, and wander back home when the sun went down. One evening their supper consisted of Linda's pet bunny, fried and plopped on the kitchen table.

> Today's confusion and crisis will be tomorrow's conquest.

Linda has no memory of her father expressing affection or even saying her name. She was able to complete high school, graduate from college, and marry a man who felt called to do mission work in Mexico. They moved to a remote area where conditions were basic and bleak. Life as a missionary was survivable. Life with her husband was not. He was an angry, abusive man. Linda feared for her life and the lives of her four children. They escaped by taking a bus to Arlington, Texas, in 1981. She arrived with one suitcase, no money, and the phone number of a friend.

She found a minimum-wage job and rented a tiny apartment. For the first three years she slept on the floor. The children shared flea market mattresses. To save money she worked through lunch each day. Since she was working while others were eating, she was more productive than her coworkers. Her manager noticed and gave her more overtime and responsibility.

Little by little she and her family stepped out of poverty. Her bosses promoted her and eventually transferred her to Houston. It was there that she came in touch with Junior Achievement. The organization exists to help kids break the cycle of poverty through education and hard work. That was Linda's story! The organization recruited her, and Linda flourished, eventually becoming the CEO of Asia Pacific and the Americas. She was responsible for fifty-five countries on five continents. Junior Achievement estimates that she affected three million lives annually and that a total of 32 million lives changed because of her influence.

But then came another challenge, ALS. I watched the disease take the life of my father. It is taking its toll on the body of Linda. But it is not taking her joy. She is still quick to smile and even quicker to thank God for her life.

"How do you do it?" I asked her. "How do you face these challenges without bitterness?"

Her answer is simple: "When you are on your own, there is only

Recast the struggle for what it is,
an opportunity for God to do again
what he does best: flip a story on its
head and resurrect life out of death.

one way to look, and that is up. People have failed me, but God never has."[6]

Could you use some of her resolve? We all could.

Take God at his word. I dare you to do so. I double dog dare you. Reframe the way you see this season of winter. Recast the struggle for what it is, an opportunity for God to do again what he does best: flip a story on its head and resurrect life out of death.

Boll weevils are no match for our good Father.

Chapter Eleven

YOU WERE MADE
FOR THIS MOMENT

When I was twelve years of age, I took on a summer responsibility of managing the houses of vacationing neighbors. It was their idea, not mine. Three families who lived side by side were planning to be out of town for a month. They each needed someone to cut their lawns, feed their pets, water their gardens. In sum they wanted to make sure their properties were cared for. They invited me to take the job. More accurately, they asked my dad to ask me to take the job. He didn't ask me. He told me. I didn't want to do it. After all, I had Little League games to play, a bike to ride, and uh, uh, uh . . . Those were the only two reasons I could muster. They got me no traction.

Before I knew it, I was sitting down with each of the families, making a list of the tasks I needed to manage on their behalf. I recall walking home from their houses feeling something I'd never felt before. I felt overwhelmed. Forgive me if my weight seems nothing compared to yours. Keep in mind, I was only twelve years old. To cut grass, feed pets, and make sure doors were locked in three households for a month? I mean, one family had a goldfish. I'd never fed a goldfish. I envisioned finding the little fellow floating on his side, dead from being under- or overfed.

But there was no getting out now.

On the first day of my unsolicited career, I hurried home from baseball practice, jumped on my bike, and pedaled like crazy to the residences. Three lawns needed mowing. Three houses needed attending. Three sets of locks needed checking. Three families had pets who needed feeding. Three gardens needed watering. This was too much for any human being to handle.

Just when I was about to learn the meaning of the phrase "panic attack," I saw it. Parked in front of the middle house. White, wide, and fresh off a day in the oil field. My dad's pickup. He was there. The garage door was open, and the lawn mower was on the driveway.

"You start cutting the grass," he said. "I'll water the plants."

With those words everything changed. The clouds lifted. I could face the task because my father was facing it with me.

Your Father wants to do the same with you.

Seasons of struggle can be a treacherous time for the human heart. We are sitting ducks for despair and defeat. We turn away from others, turn our backs on God, and turn into fearful, cynical souls. Despair can be a dangerous season. But it can also be a developing time, a time in which we learn to trust God, to lean into his Word and rely on his ways.

The choice is ours. To help us choose the wise path, God gave the wonderfully wild story of Esther. Before we wrap a ribbon on our discussion of the story, let's revisit the hinge passage in the book. Mordecai has stripped himself of his Persian disguise. For fear of the death of his people, he is the picture of anguish. He wears sackcloth and ashes. He cries out to Esther to intervene.

She resists. Dare she risk her life and make an appeal to the fickle Xerxes? Mordecai's reply is surprisingly sober.

> If you remain silent at this time, relief and deliverance for the Jews will arise from another place, but you and your father's family will perish. And who knows but that you have come to your royal position for such a time as this? (Est. 4:14)

Mordecai is not engaging in empty rah-rah rhetoric. He is deadly earnest. His message is a one-two punch: a call to faith and a call to action.

The call to faith: *Relief will come!* Did Mordecai know *how* the relief would come? Could he provide the game plan for deliverance? I see no reason to say he did. I can only assume that he stood on God's Word. He remembered God's promised deliverance of the Jewish people. God would . . .

- be their God, and they would be his people (Jer. 32:36–38).
- gather them from all the countries (Ezek. 37:24–28).
- send a king through them and to them to establish an eternal kingdom (2 Sam. 7:16; Matt. 1:21).

He recalled the covenants. Confusion? Yes. Crisis? No doubt. But above them all was the covenant-keeping character of God.

Relief will come! This was Mordecai's message for Esther. And this is God's message for you. Feeling undone by the struggle? Then let God unleash the power within you to face it. Shift your focus away from the challenges at hand, and ponder the power of your almighty God.

Do you recall the question he asked Abraham and Sarah? He promised them a son, though both were past child-bearing age. Sarah laughed at the thought of bouncing their newborn on her knee.

> Then the LORD said to Abraham, "Why did Sarah laugh? Why did she say, 'I am too old to have a baby'? Is anything too hard for the LORD?" (Gen. 18:13–14 NCV)

That is what we need to ask. Is anything too hard for God? Does he ever give up because the problem is too great? Does he ever throw up his hands and quit? Does he ever shake his head at the sound of a prayer request and say, "I can't handle that problem"?

The answer, the welcome answer, is, "No, nothing is too hard for the Lord."

You must start here. Don't measure the height of the mountain. Ponder the power of the One who made it. Don't tell God how big your storm is. Tell the storm how big your God is. Your problem is not that your problem is so big but that your view of God is too small.

Accept the invitation of the psalmist: "O magnify the Lord with me, and let us exalt his name together" (Ps. 34:3 KJV). Our tendency is to magnify our fears. We place a magnifying glass on the diagnosis, the disease, or debt.

> Your problem is not that your problem is so big but that your view of God is too small.

Stop that! Meditate less on the mess and more on the Master. Less on the problems and more on his power.

Sometimes I wonder if the church has forgotten the vastness of God. Visit a congregation on a given Sunday, and you'll likely find a group of people sitting in comfortable chairs, hearing a comforting message about a God who keeps us comfortable.

Do we know him before whom we gather? Do we understand that demons fear and flee at the sound of his name? That angels have been singing "holy, holy, holy" since creation and still haven't sung it often enough? That a glimpse of God's glory caused Isaiah, the prophet, to beg for grace and Moses, the patriarch, to duck under the protection of a rock? Do we comprehend his grandeur? His glory, fire, and power? If we did, we'd likely enter the sanctuary wearing helmets and body armor.

Are we suffering from a loss of awe? And if we are, what are the consequences?

Here's what I think. A wimpy God makes for a wimpy heart. But a great God makes for a solid saint.

Let him be big.

Meditate less on the mess

and more on the Master.

Less on the problems and

more on his power.

"'To whom will you compare me? Or who is my equal?' says the Holy One" (Isa. 40:25).

As Moses announced: "Who among the gods is like you, LORD? Who is like you—majestic in holiness?" (Ex. 15:11).

And the psalmist asked: "Who in the skies is comparable to the LORD? Who among the sons of the mighty is like the LORD?" (Ps. 89:6 NASB).

As Augustine prayed:

What then are you my God? What, I ask, except the Lord God. For who is the Lord besides God? Or who is God besides our God?—Most high, most good, most powerful, most omnipotent, most merciful and most just, most secret and most present; most beautiful and most strong; most stable and incomprehensible; unchangeable (yet) changing all things; never new, never old; making all things new, and bringing the proud to (the collapse of) old age; ever acting, ever at rest; gathering, and not needing; carrying and filling and protecting (all things); creating and nourishing and perfecting; seeking, though you lack nothing.[1]

Consider the work of his hands.

> But ask the animals, and they will teach you,
>> or ask the birds of the air, and they will tell you.
> Speak to the earth, and it will teach you,
>> or let the fish of the sea tell you.
> Every one of these knows
>> that the hand of the LORD has done this.
> The life of every creature
>> and the breath of all people are in God's hand.
>
> (JOB 12:7–10 NCV)

The next time you feel the weight of the world, talk to the One who made the world. As your perception of God grows greater, the size of your challenge grows smaller. If God can sway the heart of a Persian monarch, if he can reverse certain death into victorious life, if he can turn a scheduled holocaust into an annual holiday, do you not think he can take care of you?

I'm sorry for your exile in Persia. I'm sorry for your deep wounds and weariness. I'm so sorry that you so quickly understand the meaning of words like *pain, fear,* and *sadness.*

> The next time you feel the weight of the world, talk to the One who made the world.

Springtime seems like forever from now, I know. But, friend, it isn't. The story of Esther dares you to believe that God, though hidden, is active. He brings life out of broken things. The apostle Paul was summarizing Esther when he wrote: "And we know that in all things God works for the good of those who love him, who have been called according to his purpose" (Rom. 8:28).

"We know," Paul said. There are so many things in life we do not know. We do not know if the economy will dip or if our team will win. We don't always know what our kids are thinking or our spouse is doing. But according to Paul we can be dead certain of four things.

We know *God works.* He is busy behind the scenes, above the fray, and within the fury. He hasn't checked out or moved on. He is ceaseless and tireless.

He never stops working *for our good.* Not for our comfort, pleasure, or entertainment, but for our good. Since he himself is the ultimate good, would we expect anything else?

To do this he uses *all things. Panta* in Greek. As in *panoramic* or *panacea* or *pandemic.* All inclusive. God works, not through a few things or just the good things, best things, or easy things, but in all things God works.

He works for the good of those who love him. Good things happen to those who trust God. The umbrella of God's providence does not extend to cover the evil and hard-hearted. But for those who seek him and his will, in all things God works.

A puppet in the hands of fortune and fate? Not you. You are secure in the hands of a living and loving God. A random collection of disconnected events? Far from it. Your life is a crafted narrative written by the author of life, who is working toward your supreme good and a sublime ending.

Relief will come.

Will you be a part of it?

It seems to me that the entire world is in a state of trauma.

People do not know why they were born or where they are destined to go. This is the age of much know-how and very little know-why. The invisible enemies of sin and secularism have left us dazed and bewildered.

The world needs you! We need people with the resolve of Mordecai and the courage of Esther. The world is in desperate need of a people of God who will stay steady in the chaos.

People like the ones who gathered in war-torn London. No one would have blamed them for canceling church services on that Sunday morning. A bombing raid had roared in the city throughout the night. London was a circle of fire. Buildings were destroyed. Even the walls of this church were flattened. Members arrived to find pews covered with dust and mortar. But rather than despair, they chose to worship. Amid the heaps of stones they began to sing:

> *The church's one foundation is Jesus Christ her Lord;*
> *She is his new creation, By Spirit and the Word:*
> *From heav'n he came and sought her*

The world is in desperate need

of a people of God who will

stay steady in the chaos.

To be his holy bride,
With his own blood he bought her,
And for her life he died.

Can you envision that circle of brave souls? Smack-dab in the center of global chaos, they worshipped. They set their faith on our unfailing God. The song was an admonition of sorts, a declaration of truth amid a crumbling society.

The song may well have saved the life of Ben Robertson. He was an American war correspondent who had arrived in London the day before. The night bombing left him undone and terrified. The explosions, sirens, and cries of the wounded caused him to despair of life itself.

"If this is what modern civilization has brought us to—if this is the best that modern man can achieve, then let me die," he prayed.

At some point he dozed off. He awoke to the unexpected sound of people singing a hymn. He looked out the window and saw the congregation gathered in the rubble.

He later wrote: "Suddenly I saw in the world something that was unshatterable—something that had endured through millennia, something that was indestructible—the spirit and life and power of Jesus Christ within his church."[2]

Bombs are still dropped. Worlds still explode. Walls still collapse. Pandemics still rage. But in the midst of it all, the Lord still has his people. And when they proclaim the truth of God in the middle of a crumbling world, you never know who might be changed.

God is in the middle of this. This steep climb. This uphill struggle. This cold, fierce headwind you are facing. You feel overwhelmed. Weary. Ill-equipped to weather it. But lift up your eyes. That is your father standing on the driveway. He is in this moment with you. Who knows but that you have been chosen for such a time as this?

QUESTIONS FOR REFLECTION

Prepared by Andrea Lucado

Chapter One
SEARCHING FOR SPRINGTIME

1. In what season of life does this book find you? Winter, when you feel trapped in perpetual gloom? Summer, with its ease and warmth? Autumn, with its plentiful harvest? Or spring, which brings the hope of new life? Describe the season you're in, and why.

2. Even if you're not currently in a winter season, have you experienced winters of the heart in the past? Have you witnessed such seasons in the lives of your family or community? What kind of pain or hardship and suffering have you observed or experienced?

3. What is Max's six-letter word of encouragement for those who are in a winter season? How can Esther's story provide encouragement for the winter seasons of life?

4. Before reading this chapter what did you know about Esther and her story?
   - After you read this chapter, what facts about the time period of the book of Esther stood out to you?
   - What facts about the characters stood out to you?

5. Based on what you know so far, how would you describe King Xerxes?
   - In what ways do you relate to Esther or her circumstances?
   - How are these two characters different from each other?

6. Max describes Esther as a woman of conviction and courage. What do you have strong convictions about?
   - Think of a time when your convictions prompted you to courageous action. Explain.
   - What helped you to be courageous in this moment?
   - What do you need more of, courage or conviction, and why?

7. The book of Esther is known for what it's missing: any mention of God.
   - How does this affect the way you view the book of Esther?
   - Why do you think this book is included in the Old Testament even though it doesn't talk about God?

8. As in the book of Esther, have there been times when you felt God was absent? If so, describe a time when God felt absent or distant from you.

    • Describe a time when God felt near.

    • What makes you feel or think that God is distant? What makes you feel or think that God is near?

    • How do these feelings affect your life, your thoughts, and your relationships?

9. What is "quiet providence"? (See pp. 8–9.)

    • Why do you think God is portrayed in Scripture as speaking in a loud and booming voice and also as whispering?

    • How do you most often experience God—in dramatic interventions or quiet whispering or some other way? Describe your awareness of God's presence in your life.

    • How have these experiences affected your faith and your understanding of who God is?

10. What does Max say is the theme of the book of Esther? (See p. 9.)

    • How does God accomplish this work?

    • Max says, "God's solutions come through people of courage. . . . People who dare to believe that they, by God's grace, were made to face a moment like this" (p. 11). How would you describe the "moment" you are living in?

    • Do you see injustices that need God's intervention? In your city, community, church, or nation? Explain.

11. We are not always ready to jump into this partnering work with God. On page 9 we read: "You want to retreat, stay quiet, stay safe, stay backstage." What areas of injustice do you know about but are tempted to stay quiet and retreat from rather than participate in the work of renewal? Why do you feel this way?

    - What narratives are you believing? For example, "I don't have what it takes" (p. 9), "I'm not smart enough . . . strong enough . . . equipped or courageous enough."
    - Where do you think these narratives come from?

12. Might God be inviting you to partner with Him in helping to bring justice to your part of the world? In what area might that work be?

    - What do you need from God in order to have the courage and conviction to partner in this work?
    - What would be the ideal result of courageous action? Whom would it impact?

Chapter Two

DON'T GET COZY IN PERSIA

1. This chapter reveals more information about Persia, King Xerxes, and his wealth. Imagine what Xerxes' seven-day banquet was like.

   • Who was there?

   • What were they doing?

   • What would you have thought had you been there?

2. How did this banquet and all that Xerxes represented contrast with the way the Hebrews had been called to live?

3. Fill in the blanks: "For this reason they were to remain
_____. _____. ___. ___ _____" (p. 24).
   - Were the Israelites successful in remaining this way?
   - What did God do to get the Israelites' attention?
   - What was the result of this act?
   - By the time we get to Esther, how far removed were the Israelites from their time ruling Jerusalem?

4. Have you ever found yourself in unfamiliar territory, far from where you were raised or far from who you used to be?
   - If so, what brought you to this place?
   - How did it change you for the better?
   - How did it change you for the worse?

5. How did Xerxes reveal his true character during the seven-day banquet?
   - What does this event tell you about the leadership of Persia?
   - Does the story of the wheat-field romp remind you of a time you were attracted to something that proved untrue or disappointing? Can you relate your experience to these words: "The story of the insolent Xerxes and the story of my romp in a winter-wheat field posit the same possibility: What if the glitz and glamour are only folly and foibles? What if the lure of lights is a hoax?" How was your experience similar?

6. We can be much like the Israelites, can't we? Back and forth between loyalty and holiness and then forgetting who we are, where we came from, and what we are called to. Chronicle some of your faith journey here.

- Have you at times felt holy and steadfast in your faith? Explain.
- When have you chosen Persia over Jerusalem, staying in a place you knew wasn't good for you?
- Where are you today? Wandering in exile, or steady and close to the God you believe in, or somewhere in between? Explain your answer.

7. The church has had a journey similar to that of the Israelites—at times following the call to be holy and at times falling in line with Persia.
   - What have you witnessed in the churches you've been a part of or churches you've observed?
   - Why do you think the church's history is so rocky?
   - If you have personally experienced the church's shortcomings, how has your faith or conviction been affected? Explain.

8. "We, too, are caretakers. Caretakers of the message of Jesus" (p. 25).
   - In your own words what is the message of Jesus?
   - How could the church be a better caretaker of this message?
   - How is each believer a caretaker of this message?

9. Max lists several distractions and lies, such as pornography, alcohol, and wealth, that can prevent us from carrying the message of Jesus well. Is there any lie or deception you tend to believe that has prevented you from being the caretaker of Jesus' message that you've been called to be? If so, why does this affect the way you show God's love in the world?

10. Read 1 Peter 2:9–12.
- What does it mean to be God's "chosen people"?
- What responsibilities and gifts are inherent in being called "God's special possession"?
- What does "mercy" mean to you? How could this gift help in dealing with sinful desires that wage war against our souls?
- Why does mercy move us to "live such good lives" that it benefits those around us?

11. When you hear the phrase "Take a stand for your faith or what you believe in," what comes to mind?
- What does this phrase mean to you?
- Where did this understanding come from?
- According to 1 Peter 2:9–12, taking a stand or keeping our post, as Max did when he was on first-aid duty at Boy Scout camp, starts with the sin in our own hearts and how we deal with it. How does this compare to your previous understanding of taking a stand?
- If this is how we take a stand, how could the church do a better job of it?

Chapter Three
THE GIRL WITH TWO NAMES

1. Max shares a story from his adolescence when he decided to conform rather than transform as Romans 12:2 calls us to do.
   - Did you ever conform as an adolescent in an attempt to cover up who you truly were?
   - If so, describe that experience. How did it make you feel?

2. The temptation to conform doesn't cease with childhood. Even as adults we want to fit in and belong.
   - Have you ever conformed as an adult?
   - If so, why did you conform?

- What part of your true self were you covering up, and why were you ashamed of this part of yourself?

3. Who conformed in the story of Esther?
   - Does it trouble you to know this? (p. 34). Explain your response.
   - Why do you think the Bible is full of characters who conformed, ran from God, killed their brothers, committed adultery, etc.?

4. What was significant about Mordecai's conforming to Persian culture?
   - Where did he live?
   - Where did he work?
   - What does the name "Mordecai" mean?
   - Why was Mordecai's life so defiant of the Hebrew call to separateness? Why do you think he went against this call and blended in?

5. Can you empathize with Mordecai?
   - Have you ever conformed to the place where you lived or worked? In what ways?
   - Have you changed your name for the sake of fitting in?
   - If so, what thoughts or feelings did you have during this time?
   - How did this conforming affect the way you felt about yourself?
   - How did it affect your faith?

6. What Esther had to go through to win favor from King Xerxes is cringeworthy. As Max said, "The girls were not asked to love him, just entertain him" (p. 36).

- What does this gathering of beautiful virgins tell you about King Xerxes' character?
- What does this tell you about the Persian culture of the time?
- Why do you think Mordecai and Esther went through with it?
- How do you think Esther felt about her time with the king?

7. Early on, Mordecai and Esther hid their heritage.
   - Has this ever been your initial response to a situation? If so, describe what that experience was like for you.
   - Why was your knee-jerk reaction to cover up who you truly were?
   - What was the result?

8. Max theorizes why Mordecai allowed his cousin to be sent to Xerxes.
   - What is your theory?
   - If you had been Mordecai, living in Persia, three generations removed from Babylonian exile, would you have done the same? Why or why not?

9. "The incontestable value of Western culture is tolerance. Ironically, the champions of tolerance are intolerant of a religion like Christianity that adheres to one Savior and one solution to the human problem" (p. 40).
   - Does this ring true for you in your context—where you live, where you worship, who your friends are? Why or why not?
   - Have you personally experienced hostility from others because you are a Christian? Or have you witnessed

this elsewhere? If so, has this tempted you to do what Max did at the beginning of this chapter and "peel off the sweatshirt" and deny your faith?

- How did this experience make you feel about yourself, about God, and about your faith?

10. For many evangelical Christians the word *tolerance* has a negative connotation.
    - Is there a positive or loving way to express tolerance in our world today as Christians?
    - If so, what could that look like?
    - How do you hope those around you will tolerate your religion? How could you tolerate parts of their identity you may not agree with?

11. Reread the story of the tree at the end of the chapter and consider:
    - What did this heart signify to Max when he saw it?
    - How is this a metaphor for our own identity?
    - How is this a metaphor for God's love for us?

12. First John 3:1 says, "What marvelous love the Father has extended to us! Just look at it—we're called children of God! That's who we really are" (THE MESSAGE).
    - Do you believe this about yourself?
    - It's easy to give the right answer—yes—but what do you really believe about yourself?
    - How could God meet you in this belief today? How could you talk to him about it?

Chapter Four

HE REFUSED
TO BOW

1. This chapter shares the tragic, yet moving, account of the men
   who died at the hands of ISIS because of their Christian faith.
   - Do you remember hearing about this event or another
     incident in which people died for what they believed?
   - If so, what was your reaction? What questions did it
     raise in your mind?
   - How did it affect you?

2. Ponder this: "You may not face blades and terrorists, but don't
   you face critics and accusers?" (p. 51).

- Have you faced critics or accusers of your faith? If so, how did these critiques affect you and your faith?
- Perhaps you come from a supportive community that doesn't criticize your beliefs, but what have you been criticized for? Values, cultural traditions, or other important parts of your identity?
- How did these critiques affect the way you felt about yourself?

3. What is significant about Haman's ancestry?
     - Do you believe racism can be passed down from one generation to another? If so, how have you seen this play out in your community or elsewhere or maybe even in yourself?
     - What other sins have you seen passed down through generations?
     - Why do you think bloodlines and ethnicities sometimes repeat the sins of their forebearers?

4. Esther 3:2 says, "All the royal officials at the king's gate knelt down and paid honor to Haman, for the king had commanded this concerning him. But Mordecai would not kneel down or pay him honor."
     - Imagine the scene. What might have been the crowd's reaction to Mordecai's disobedience?
     - Has your heart ever prompted you to an action that might have appeared to be disobedience but in reality represented your deepest conviction? Explain.
     - How did Mordecai's action propel the subsequent events of the story?

5. Why did Mordecai choose this moment to reveal his identity as a Jew?
    - Have you ever encountered a turning point like this, when you decided enough was enough, and you had to be true to who you were? If so, describe that experience.
    - How can being honest about our identity give us courage to stand up for ourselves, for others, and for what we believe in?
    - How can hiding our true selves make taking stands like this difficult, if not impossible?

6. Mordecai was the only Jew who refused to bow to Haman. Why do you think Haman's response was to kill every Jew in the nation?

7. After couriers sent out the decree that every Jew would be killed, Scripture says Haman and Xerxes sat down for a drinking spree. Why do you think they were able to have such disregard for human life in that moment?
    - How do positions of power enable us to turn a blind eye toward injustice?
    - What injustice have you been able to ignore because of your position in society, your ethnicity, your class, etc.?
    - What injustice have you not been able to ignore because of your position in society, your ethnicity, your class, etc.?

8. This chapter reminds us, "Resistance matters" (p. 59).
    - How would you define resistance in this context?

- Have you ever witnessed resistance like this? If so, what was it like to watch someone resist?
- Have you ever resisted someone or something or some institution? If so, what was that experience like for you?

9. While your opportunities to stand up for your faith and against injustice may not be extreme, as Max says, "Chances are high that you'll be tempted to compromise your beliefs or to remain silent in the face of injustice and evil" (p. 57).
   - Have you ever been tempted to remain silent in the face of injustice? If so, what made it difficult to speak up?
   - Have you ever resisted this temptation and spoken up anyway? If so, how did that feel? What was the result?
   - What gave you the courage to say something?

10. Think of others aside from Mordecai who have taken bold stands for their beliefs, such as the former Nazi Party member who refused to salute Hitler, and Shadrach, Meshach, and Abednego, who refused to worship a Babylonian idol.
    - Describe someone you have seen take a bold stand. What did this person do?
    - How did his or her courage inspire you?
    - What situation are you facing that calls for more courage?
    - Why are you afraid to speak up? What is holding you back?
    - Set a time today to talk to God about this.

Chapter Five

RELIEF WILL COME

1. Esther 4:1–2 describes the dire state Mordecai was in after Xerxes agreed to the extermination of the Jews: "When Mordecai learned of all that had been done, he tore his clothes, put on sackcloth and ashes, and went out into the city, wailing loudly and bitterly. But he went only as far as the king's gate, because no one clothed in sackcloth was allowed to enter it."

   - Have you ever felt the type of pain and grief Mordecai was experiencing? If so, what caused this pain?
   - You probably didn't wear sackcloth, but what, if any, outward signs of grief did you display?

2. What was Esther's initial response to Mordecai's plea to help their people? (See Esther 4:11.)

- Why do you think she responded this way?
- Have you ever hesitated before doing the right thing? If so, what were the circumstances? Why did you hesitate?

3. Read Mordecai's response to Esther's hesitation in Esther 4:13–14:

Do not think that because you are in the king's house you alone of all the Jews will escape. For if you remain silent at this time, relief and deliverance for the Jews will arise from another place, but you and your father's family will perish. And who knows but that you have come to your royal position for such a time as this?

- Max says Mordecai made two astute observations in these verses. What are they?
- What protection was Esther trusting that Mordecai called out as untrue?
- Have you ever clung to a promise God never made to you? If so, what was that promise, and how did believing in it affect your faith and your actions?
- What promise did Jesus make to all of us in John 16:33?
- How would you answer Max's question regarding this promise: "Does your view of God include a certain relief and dramatic deliverance?" (p. 72). Explain your answer.
- In what area of your life do you need relief and deliverance today?

4. Mordecai told Esther that perhaps she had come to her royal position for such a time as this. Do you believe God places us in certain places at certain times?

- If so, have you experienced this in your own life? Explain how.

- If not, have you ever witnessed or heard of this happening to someone else? What did you think of that person's experience?

5. Mordecai has undergone a transformation since we met him in the second chapter of Esther. Explain how he has changed.
   - What is Max's explanation for Mordecai's transformation? (See p. 71.)
   - Has God ever awakened you to a suppressed belief? If so, what did that feel like?
   - How did you or your life change as a result?
   - What might God be moving you to reexamine now?

6. Esther also undergoes a transformation in this chapter. What is the turning point for her? (See Esther 4:16.)
   - What do you think caused her to change so dramatically?
   - At the end of verse 16, after making her decision to fast and then visit the king, Esther boldly declares, "And if I perish, I perish." Have you ever felt this resolute about something? You knew it was the right thing to do even if it meant sacrificing something dear to you. If so, what made you feel that resolve?
   - What was the outcome?

7. Esther's "such a time as this" was being in a position of power when the lives of her people were threatened the most.
   - What is your "such a time as this" right now or, as Max describes it, the holy work you've been invited to participate in? What has God been preparing you for?
   - How has he equipped you to handle this work?
   - How are you feeling in the face of this holy work?

Do you feel as Esther did when she was hesitant to act, or do you feel as Esther did when she resolved to perish if necessary? Why?

- Do you need to be reminded of the question Max poses: "But what if God is in this?" (p. 75).
- Where have you already seen God in this work?
- Where have you seen him in past seasons like this, and how could that give you hope for your current invitation to participate in God's holy work?

Chapter Six
TWO THRONE ROOMS

1. Fill in the blanks: "Rather than rush into the throne room of Xerxes, she _____ herself and stepped into ___ _____ ____ __ ___."

   • Why do you think Esther chose to fast for three days before approaching Xerxes?
   • What role does prayer play in the big decisions or moments of your life, and why?

2. By this point in the story, Esther is in a position of power. She could have chosen to ignore the decree to kill the Jews, as it

might not affect her directly. Yet she chose to act. How can power and status breed apathy in us?

- What problems or issues do you feel apathetic about?
- Why do you feel apathetic about these issues?
- How do we move from apathy to empathy even when a problem does not directly affect us?
- How did Esther do this?

3. What happened when Esther entered Xerxes' throne room? (See Esther 5:2.)

- Why do you think Xerxes responded this way?
- Have your prayers ever led to an unexpected answer? If so, explain what happened.
- How did this event affect your faith?

4. What role did humility play in Esther's course of action with Xerxes?

- What role does humility play in partnering with God's holy work?
- Have you ever been humbled in a way that led you to action? If so, how did humility encourage you to act or do what you felt God was calling you to?
- How has a lack of humility prevented you from doing what God called you to do?

5. Daniel is a model of someone in Scripture who prayed with humility. Read his prayer in Daniel 9:17–18 about the end of captivity for the Israelites:

So listen, God, to this determined prayer of your servant. Have mercy on your ruined Sanctuary. Act out of who you are, not out of what we are.

Turn your ears our way, God, and listen. Open your eyes

and take a long look at our ruined city, this city named after you. We know that we don't deserve a hearing from you. Our appeal is to your compassion. This prayer is our last and only hope. (THE MESSAGE)

- Underline any words or phrases that display humility toward God.
- What do you need to pray about that you haven't been praying about?
- Why haven't you been praying about this?
- How could you approach God's throne room with humility today?

6. Max shares his conviction to speak out against racism, especially the history of racism in the church. His reason for not doing this before might sound familiar: "But I'm not a racist. I've done nothing wrong against the Black community. I've never spoken against African Americans" (p. 87). What clear word did he hear from God after this?

- How can our silence be hurtful when it comes to racism or other social problems?
- Have you ever wrestled with whether to speak up for a certain person or people group? If so, what was your reason for not speaking up?

7. Read Max's prayer on pages 87–88.
- What caught your attention, and why?
- What, if anything, bothered you about his prayer, and why?
- What, if anything, in this prayer convicted you, and why?
- What would you repent of if you were to pray a public prayer of repentance?

- How would it feel to be honest about this repentance?
- Why was it important for Max to pray this specific prayer? What impact did it have?

8. On what subject do you need to have a "no-nonsense, honest, face-on-the-floor talk with the Lord"? Spend some time in prayer about this now. You can do this silently or out loud, or write down the words of your prayer if that's helpful. Approach God's throne with an attitude of humility, and see how this changes your words and requests.

Chapter Seven

GOD IS LOUDEST WHEN HE WHISPERS

1. What do you think of the butterfly effect—the idea that humans are the victims of chance?
   - What do you think about the idea of God's providence?
   - What role do you believe God plays in the events of your life?
   - Where did this belief come from?
   - Has it changed over the years? If so, how and why?

2. Even if you don't fully believe in or understand God's will and how he orchestrates it, have you ever had an experience that was beyond coincidence? A time when events fell into place in

such a way that you knew someone divine had to be behind it? If so, explain what happened. How did witnessing this affect your faith?

3. After the dinner with King Xerxes and Esther, Haman was in a good mood until he saw Mordecai. He said, "All this gives me no satisfaction as long as I see that Jew Mordecai sitting at the king's gate" (Est. 5:13).
   - Why do you think Mordecai had such a strong effect on Haman?
   - What did Haman decide to do to Mordecai as a result?
   - Why do you think his response was so extreme?

4. The stage was set for Mordecai's execution, but a series of events changed Mordecai's fate.
   - What were those events?
   - How did each event affect the others?
   - What happened to Mordecai as a result?
   - What does this series of events tell you about God's involvement in this story?
   - What does it tell you about God's involvement in our lives?

5. What was Mordecai's role in these events that ultimately saved his life? What kind of control did he have over them?
   - What does this tell you about the control we have over our lives?
   - What does this tell you about the value of integrity?

6. Have you or someone close to you ever been wrongfully accused of something? If so, explain what happened.
   - What makes such experiences so painful?

- Did you try to correct the false accusation? If so, how, and what happened?
- What does Mordecai's story tell you about God's role in maintaining the integrity and name of his people?

7. Max asks, "Do you think the odds are against you? That even God is against you? You've been led to believe that life is a roll of the dice, and you can't remember the last time they rolled in your favor?" (p. 102). Do these questions resonate with you? If so, what events in your life have led you to believe God or fate is against you?

8. How were you affected by the story of a mother who had been contemplating suicide? What events led her to read *Tell Me the Story*, and what happened as a result?
   - What part of the story touched you most?
   - Where do you see the hand of God in the mother's life and the lives of her children?
   - Have you ever encountered God after a long season in which you hadn't felt his presence? If so, describe that experience.

9. Max also shares the story of Russian writer Aleksandr Solzhenitsyn. What events led him to encounter a recently converted doctor, and what happened as a result?
   - What do you think of this story, particularly that Solzhenitsyn had renounced his faith before this encounter happened?
   - Where do you see the hand of God on his life?
   - Have you ever encountered God during a time you didn't think you even believed in him? If so, describe that experience.

10. It is difficult to believe that God is in the details when we are in a season of doubt or difficulty. Max suggests that even during times like this you should "assume that God is at work. Move forward as if God is moving forward in your life. Give no quarter to the voices of doubt and fear. Don't cower to the struggle" (p. 107).

- What if you really believed God was moving forward in your life? How would that change your actions, your thoughts, and your faith?
- In what area of your life do you most need this belief? What would you do next if you truly believed God was already at work?

Chapter Eight
THE WICKED WILL NOT WIN

1. Who is a Haman in your life? Someone who is small-minded or self-centered? Someone who gets under your skin? This can be someone you know personally or someone you know about.
   - How do you feel about this person?
   - What do you think it would take for this person to change?

2. Esther's words to King Xerxes turned this story around for good:

   If I have found favor with you, Your Majesty, and if it pleases you, grant me my life—this is my petition. And spare my people—this is my request. For I and my people have been sold to be destroyed, killed and annihilated. If we had merely been sold as male and female slaves, I would have kept quiet, because no such distress would justify disturbing the king. (Est. 7:3–4)

- What is significant about Esther's language in this passage?
- How do you think she felt as she revealed to the king and to Haman her true identity as a Jew?
- What moment in your life convicted you to speak up about who you truly are or what you believe?
- How did it feel to reveal this part of yourself?

3. What happened to Haman during this act of the story?
   - How did you respond to this part of Haman's narrative?
   - Why do you think it is satisfying to see the bad guy get what he deserves?
   - What does Haman's fate tell you about the nature of God?
   - Have you witnessed this type of fairness or justice in your own life? If so, how was justice achieved?

4. Fill in the blanks from Romans 11:22: "Consider therefore the _____ and _____ of God."
   - How do you feel about describing God as kind?
   - How do you feel about describing God as stern?
   - Why must God be both?

5. It's satisfying to see Haman's evil revealed and to watch him being taken into custody (Est. 7:8). But as you know, justice doesn't always happen so quickly in our lives. What act of justice are you waiting for?

- Where do you think God is in the process of restoring this justice?
- How do you wait? With patience, anxiety, or questions? Explain your answer.

6. Scripture is not silent on the topic of waiting for God's judgment to restore justice. Read the following passages:

O Lord, how long will you look on? (Ps. 35:17 GW)

Why does the way of the wicked prosper? (Jer. 12:1)

Truth is nowhere to be found,
   and whoever shuns evil becomes a prey.
The LORD looked and was displeased
   that there was no justice.
He saw that there was no one,
   he was appalled that there was no one to intervene. (Isa. 59:15–16)

7. Scripture is also not silent on the topic of what God will ultimately do about injustice. Read the following passages:

He will judge everyone according to what they have done. (Rom. 2:6 NLT)

[God] has set a day when he will judge the world. (Acts 17:31)

God is a just judge,
And God is angry with the wicked every day. (Ps. 7:11 NKJV)

8. What have we been called to do while we wait for God to bring his righteous judgment? (See Isaiah 58:6–8.)
    - How can you be a facilitator of justice in your own life today and with those around you?
    - How did Charles Mulli create justice in his community?
    - How did his upbringing make him well suited for this type of work?

9. We can feel overwhelmed by the desperate need for justice around us. It can be difficult to pinpoint how to partner with God in this work. Charles Mulli is a good example of someone who decided to work in the area that hit close to home for him.
    - What hits close to home for you? What injustice do you see in the world that breaks your heart?
    - Why does this particular thing break your heart?
    - What steps could you take to start partnering with God in this area, whether it's feeding the homeless, visiting a home for the elderly in your community, helping kids to get off the street, or something else?

Chapter Nine

THE GOD OF GREAT TURNAROUNDS

1. What do you think Dalia and Ayesha expected to happen if Ayesha's husband discovered she had been reading the Bible? What happened instead?
   - How do you think they expected him to respond to the Jesus film? How did he respond instead?
   - How do you think these unexpected responses affected Dalia and Ayesha and their faith in Christianity?

2. Fill in the blanks: "God is the God of the ____ _____" (p. 129). How did the Jews' fate change in this chapter?

3. What role did Xerxes play in this plot twist for the Jews and their fate?
    - Why is it so surprising he would behave in this way?
    - Is there an authority figure in your life right now whom you fear, or do you feel that you're at the mercy of a boss or teacher, parent or politician? If so, who is this person, and what kind of power does he or she have over your life?
    - How could Xerxes' change of heart change the way you view this authority figure in your life?

4. Xerxes listened to Esther, he had Haman arrested and bound for the gallows, and he elevated Mordecai to be his right-hand man, but the Jews were still facing a death sentence.
    - Have you ever faced a seemingly insurmountable obstacle in your life? As Max asks, "Are you staring at an unscalable wall or impossible challenge?" (p. 130). If so, what is that challenge?
    - Why does it seem impossible to overcome?
    - How did Esther and Xerxes ultimately work around the king's edict to exterminate the Jews in Persia?
    - What creative solutions could God have in store for your problem?

5. What is peripety?
    - How did Mordecai experience peripety in this story?
    - How did Esther experience peripety?
    - How did Xerxes experience peripety?
    - How did God's people experience peripety?

6. In your life have you experienced unexpected turnarounds? If so, make a list, acknowledging the hand of God in each event.

Consider drawing a time line of your life and marking those instances when something unexpected happened to change the course of your life.

- How does it feel to examine the plot twists of your life?
- What does this tell you about the character of God?
- What does this tell you about his plans for your life?

7. Max compares Esther 4:3 with Esther 8:16:

   Esther 4:3: "There was great mourning among the Jews, with fasting, weeping and wailing. Many lay in sackcloth and ashes."

   Esther 8:16: "For the Jews it was a time of happiness and joy, gladness and honor."

8. Max lists several moments of peripety in Scripture, but what was the greatest one?

- What did that moment of peripety represent?
- What does it tell you about the resurrection and restoration that is possible in your own life?
- In what area today do you need the hope of resurrection?
- How can Christ provide that hope?

9. We are often on the receiving end of plot twists when God works a miracle in our lives. But we can also provide these moments for others. How did Stan Mooneyham and World Vision turn things around for Vinh Chung and his family?

- Max poses two questions at the end of this chapter: "Are you in need of rescue? Are you available to rescue someone else?" (p. 138). How would you answer these questions?

- What do you think it takes to be available to rescue someone else?
- Are you ready for that work if God calls you to it? Why or why not?
- If you're in need of rescue, how could you pray for that today?
- If you want to be available to rescue others, how could you ask God to prepare you for that work?

Chapter Ten

A PURIM PEOPLE

1. Why is the boll weevil memorialized on a statue in Alabama?

2. What are the boll weevils in your life right now? What's causing distress or destruction but feels impossible to overcome?
   - How has this "pest" affected your day-to-day life?
   - How has this "pest" affected your faith?

3. What were the boll weevils in Esther's story, and what did she and Mordecai ultimately do with them? What does this tell you about the pests we encounter in our lives?

4. What is the feast of Purim, how is it celebrated, and who celebrates it?

- Why do you think Mordecai called for all the Jews throughout the provinces to remember this day?
- Why is remembering events like this important?
- Are there days—religious, cultural, or personal—that you remember in a special way?
- Why and how do you celebrate these days?

5. Max says, "I appreciate the value of a two-day celebration in which people of faith revisit the day and way their God prevailed. We tend to forget. We tend to forget that God is for us, not against us" (p. 144).

- Why is God's faithfulness so easy for us to forget?
- What happens when you forget that God is for you? How does this affect your behavior, your interactions with others, and your interactions with God?

6. Consider the story of J. J. Cohen reading the Purim story to his fellow Auschwitz prisoners. By the end of the story, Cohen writes, "And like a river overflowing its banks, the festive atmosphere and the vision of redemption burst out of the broken hearts of the camp inmates" (p. 145).

- What story has given you hope like this? Was it something from Scripture, a movie, a book, a friend's story?
- Why did this story give you so much hope?
- Why do stories have such a powerful effect on us?

7. Each Sunday in many Christian churches we remember the night before Jesus' crucifixion by reading the words he spoke to his disciples at the Last Supper:

Jesus took some bread, gave thanks, broke it, and gave it to the apostles, saying, "This is my body, which I am giving for you. Do this to remember me." In the same way, after supper, Jesus took the cup and said, "This cup is the new agreement that God makes with his people. This new agreement begins with my blood which is poured out for you." (Luke 22:19–20 NCV)

- What is the significance of partaking of Communion on the first day of the week?
- Why did Jesus ask his disciples to do these things to remember him?
- If you partake in Communion or Eucharist, what does it mean to you?
- What do the bread and wine represent?

8. The disciples didn't see any good coming out of the crucifixion. They thought their teacher was gone forever. Then what happened?
    - How did Christ's death turn into an opportunity for God's power?
    - How could the difficulties you face right now be an opportunity for God's power to work in your life?
    - How have you seen this happen before?
    - How could remembering those moments give you hope for your current circumstances?

9. Remembrance was a big theme in this chapter. What moments of God's faithfulness could you begin to commemorate? Your last chemotherapy treatment or the job offer you thought would never come or the day you met Christ? How could you commemorate this day in a meaningful way?

Chapter Eleven

YOU WERE MADE FOR THIS MOMENT

1. Max shares the story of being twelve years old and feeling overwhelmed by his summer job of house-sitting for three families. What made him feel better his first day on the job?

    - Has someone's presence ever made you go from feeling overwhelmed by a task to believing you could do it? If so, who was this person, and how did his or her presence ease your mind or bring you the help you needed?

    - What are the differences in facing something difficult alone and facing it with someone by your side?

2. Read the "hinge passage" of this book again:

> If you remain silent at this time, relief and deliverance for the Jews will arise from another place, but you and your father's family will perish. And who knows but that you have come to your royal position for such a time as this? (Est. 4:14)

   - Fill in the blanks: Mordecai's message is a one-two punch: a call to ____ and a call to _____.
   - What is the promise made to Esther and Mordecai regarding their people?
   - What allowed Mordecai to have faith in this promise?

3. How would you explain in your own words the covenant-keeping character of God?
   - What promises has he kept for you?
   - What promises has he kept for those you know?
   - What are some examples in Scripture of God keeping his promises?
   - What covenant promise of God do you need to believe today in order to face what feels overwhelming?

4. When it comes to our fears and struggles, where must we start, according to Max? (See p. 156.)
   - When you look at your "mountain," how big is it? How difficult is it, and why?
   - When you look at God, how big is he? Or how small is he, and why?
   - Have you suffered from "a loss of awe" (p. 156)? If so, what have been the consequences for you?

5. How did God prove his power through the life of Esther?
   - How did God prove his power through the life of Mordecai?

- How did God prove his power through the changed heart of Xerxes?
- How did God prove his power through the justice done to Haman?
- Which of these examples gives you the most hope for God's ability and willingness to prove his power in your life today, and why?

6. Read Augustine's words below. Underline every word used to describe God.

   What then are you my God? What, I ask, except the Lord God. For who is the Lord besides God? Or who is God besides our God?—Most high, most good, most powerful, most omnipotent, most merciful and most just, most secret and most present; most beautiful and most strong; most stable and incomprehensible; unchangeable (yet) changing all things; never new, never old; making all things new, and bringing the proud to (the collapse of) old age; ever acting, ever at rest; gathering, and not needing; carrying and filling and protecting (all things); creating and nourishing and perfecting; seeking, though you lack nothing.[1]

   - Which of these descriptions stood out to you, and why?
   - Which ones directly apply to what you are facing now, and why?

7. Paul wrote in a letter to the Romans: "And we know that in all things God works for the good of those who love him, who have been called according to his purpose" (Rom. 8:28).
   - Why is this verse so meaningful for some people and so challenging for others?
   - Have there been times in your life when this verse has been your mainstay? Explain.
   - How would you explain this verse to a new believer?

8. During the course of reading this book, where have you seen God in your difficult season or in your struggles?
   - Have you been more aware of his presence? If so, how?
   - Could it be that God brought you to this book for such a time as this? If so, what have you learned that you will take with you and remember during times of struggle?
   - What could you immediately put into practice?

NOTES

Chapter 1: Searching for Springtime

1. "Map of the Persian Empire," Bible Study, https://www.biblestudy.org/maps/persian-empire-at-its-height.html.
2. Google maps, "Punjab, India to Khartoum," https://www.google.com/maps/dir/Punjab,+India/Khartoum/@23.9472385,34.6168536,4z/data=!3m1!4b1!4m15!4m14!1m5!1m1!1s0x391964aa569e7355:0x8fbd263103a38861!2m2!1d75.3412179!2d31.1471305!1m5!1m1!1s0x168e8fde9837cabf:0x191f55de7e67db40!2m2!1d32.5598994!2d15.5006544!3e2!4e1.
3. Karen H. Jobes, *Esther*, The NIV Application Commentary (Grand Rapids, MI: Zondervan, 1999), 28.
4. Jobes, *Esther*, 96.
5. The other book is Song of Songs.

Chapter 2: Don't Get Cozy in Persia

1. Karen H. Jobes, *Esther*, The NIV Application Commentary (Grand Rapids, MI: Zondervan, 1999), 60.
2. Mike Cosper, *Faith Among the Faithless: Learning from Esther How to Live in a World Gone Mad* (Nashville, TN: Nelson Books, 2018), 3.

3. Jobes, *Esther*, 61. "He . . . found 40,000 talents of gold and silver bullion (1,200 tons) and 9,000 talents of minted gold coins (270 tons)." Assuming one ton of gold is worth $45,500,000 x 1,200 tons = $54.6 billion.

4. Rabbi Avie Gold, *Purim: Its Observance and Significance* (Brooklyn, NY: Mesorah Publications, 1991), 99.

5. Esther 1:1.

6. Ezra 2:1–2; 3:8.

7. Ezra 7:1, 9.

8. Fiona MacRae, "Brain Scans Prove Porn Is as Addictive as Alcohol and Drugs," *Daily Mail*, September 23, 2013, https://www.news.com .au/lifestyle/relationships/brain-scans-prove-porn-is-as-addictive-as -alcohol-and-drugs/news-story/079a1c68c1e5823aec75fe769113dc86.

9. Uplift Families, "Pornography Changes the Brain," June 16, 2015, https://www.upliftfamilies.org/pornography_changes_the_brain.

10. Erin El Issa, "2020 American Household Credit Card Debt Study," Nerdwallet's, January 12, 2021, https://www.nerdwallet.com/blog /average-credit-card-debt-household/.

11. John Stonestreet and Brett Kunkle, *A Practical Guide to Culture: Helping the Next Generation Navigate Today's World* (Colorado Springs, CO: David C. Cook, 2017, 2020), 242–43.

12. "Alcohol Use and Your Health," Centers for Disease Control and Prevention, February 23, 2021, https://www.cdc.gov/alcohol/fact -sheets/alcohol-use.htm.

13. "Depression Symptoms Rise During Covid-19 Pandemic," *Physician's Weekly*, September 8, 2020, https://www.physiciansweekly.com /depression-symptoms-rise-during-covid-19-pandemic.

14. Lauren Edmonds, "Divorce Rates in America Soar 34% during COVID; Surge Not Unexpected, Says Rose Law Group Partner and Family Law Director Kaine Fisher," Rose Law Group Reporter, https://roselawgroupreporter.com/2020/08/divorce-rates-in-america -soar-34-during-covid/.

15. Amanda Jackson, "A Crisis Mental-Health Hotline Has Seen an 891% Spike in Calls," CNN, April 10, 2020, cnn.com/2020/04/10/us/disaster -hotline-call-increase-wellness-trnd/index.html.

16. Jamie Ducharme, "U. S. Suicide Rates Are the Highest They've Been Since World War II," *Time*, June 20, 2019, https://time.com/5609124 /us-suicide-rate-increase/.

17. Ryan Prior, "1 in 4 Young People Are Reporting Suicidal Thoughts.

Here's How to Help," CNN, August 15, 2020, https://www.cnn
.com/2020/08/14/health/young-people-suicidal-ideation-wellness
/index.html.

Chapter 3: The Girl with Two Names

1. Joyce G. Baldwin, *Esther: An Introduction and Commentary*, Tyndale
   Old Testament Commentaries (Downers Grove, IL: InterVarsity,
   1984), 66.
2. Karen H. Jobes, *Esther, The NIV Application Commentary* (Grand
   Rapids, MI: Zondervan, 1999), 110.
3. Yoram Hazony, *God and Politics in Esther* (New York: Cambridge
   University Press, 2016), 18.
4. Iain M. Duguid, *Esther and Ruth,* Reformed Expository Commentary
   (Phillipsburg, NJ: P&R Publishing, 2005), 21.
5. Rabbi Meir in the *William Davidson Talmud*, Megillah 13a, p. 4,
   https://www.sefaria.org/Megillah.13a?lang=bi.
6. Duguid, *Esther and Ruth*, 21; Jobes, *Esther*, 96.

Chapter 4: He Refused to Bow

1. Nabeel Qureshi, "What Does Jesus Have to Do with ISIS?" *Christian
   Post*, March 13, 2016, https://www.christianpost.com/news/what-does
   -jesus-have-to-do-with-isis.html.
2. Jaren Malsin, "Christians Mourn Their Relatives Beheaded by ISIS,"
   Time, February 23, 2015, https://time.com/3718470/isis-copts-egypt/.
3. "I will pay $20,000,000 into the royal treasury . . . " (Esther 3:9 TLB).
4. Rabbi Avie Gold, *Purim: Its Observance and Significance* (Brooklyn,
   NY: Mesorah Publications, 1991), 109.
5. Jenn Gidman, "Tragic Tale of the German Who Wouldn't Salute
   Hitler," *USA Today*, July 3, 2015, https://www.usatoday.com/story
   /news/world/2015/07/03/german-no-salute-hitler-ex-nazi/29662195/;
   Alex Q. Arbuckle, "1936, The Man Who Folded His Arms: The Story
   of August Landmesser," https://mashable.com/2016/09/03/august
   -landmesser.
6. Gold, *Purim*, 47.
7. Thomas Philipose, "What Made a Non Believer Chadian Citizen
   Die for Christ, Along with His '20 Coptic Christian Friends'?"
   Malankara Orthodox Syrian Church, Diocese of Bombay,
   February 22, 2015, https://web.archive.org/web/20150312223941/
   http://bombayorthodoxdiocese.org/what-made-a-non-believer-chadian

-citizen-die-for-christ-along-with-his-20-coptic-christian-friends/; Stefan
J. Bos, "African Man Turns to Christ Moments Before Beheading,"
BosNewsLife, April 23, 2015, https://www.bosnewslife.com/2015
/04/23/african-man-turns-to-christ-moments-before-beheading
/#comments. Nabeel Qureshi, "What Does Jesus Have to Do with
ISIS?"

Chapter 5: Relief Will Come

1. Jeff Kelly Lowenstein, "How a Little-Known Incident in 1956
   Unnerved MLK," CNN, January 15, 2021, https://www.cnn.com
   /2021/01/15/opinions/martin-luther-king-jr-crisis-of-faith-lowenstein
   /index.html.

Act 3: Conquest

1. Yoram Hazony, *God and Politics in Esther* (New York: Cambridge
   University Press, 2016), 241. In the Midrash—a Jewish commentary
   on some of the Hebrew text—Mordecai saw three children who gave
   him three passages, starting with "Be not afraid of the sudden terror,
   neither of the destruction of the wicked when it comes" (Prov. 3:25).
   The second followed, saying, "Take counsel together, and it will be
   brought to naught. Speak the word and it will not stand, for God is
   with us" (Isa. 8:10). Then the third spoke up with the verse "Even to
   old age I am the same, and to silver hair will I carry you. I have made
   this and I will bear. I will carry and I will deliver" (Isa. 46:4).

Chapter 7: God Is Loudest When He Whispers

1. "The Butterfly Effect: Everything You Need to Know About This
   Powerful Mental Model," Farnam Street fs (blog), https://fs.blog/2017
   /08/the-butterfly-effect/.
2. Some rabbinic sources say that Haman had to take on the role of
   Mordecai's personal servant and as such was responsible for lowering
   himself so Mordecai could step on his neck to mount the horse!
3. David Aikman, *Great Souls: Six Who Changed the Century*
   (Nashville, TN: Word, 1998), 128–52.
4. Aleksandr Solzhenitsyn, *The Gulag Archipelago 1918–56: An
   Experiment in Literary Investigation*, trans. Thomas P. Whitney and
   Harry Willets, abr. Edward E. Ericson, Jr. (London: Harvill Press,
   1986), 309–10.
5. Solzhenitsyn, *The Gulag Archipelago,* 312.

Chapter 8: The Wicked Will Not Win

1. "Four O'Clock," *The Twilight Zone,* Wikipedia, https://twilightzone .fandom.com/wiki/Four_O%27Clock and https://en.wikipedia.org /wiki/Four_O%27Clock_(The_Twilight_Zone).

2. John Phillips, *Exploring the Book of Daniel: An Expository Commentary* (Grand Rapids, MI: Kregel, 2004), 85.

3. Edward W. Goodrick and John R. Kohlenberger III, *The NIV Exhaustive Concordance* (Grand Rapids, MI: Zondervan, 1990), "wrath" 1276–77, "mercy" 748–49.

4. Kara Bettis, "How the 'World's Largest Family' Survived a Global Pandemic," *Christianity Today,* November 23, 2020, https://www .christianitytoday.com/ct/2020/december/charles-mulli-childrens -worlds-largest-family-covid.htm.

Chapter 9: The God of Great Turnarounds

1. From a personal conversation with the author. Used by permission.

2. Vinh Chung with Tim Downs, *Where the Wind Leads: A Refugee Family's Miraculous Story of Loss, Rescue, and Redemption* (Nashville, TN: W Publishing, 2014), 3–4.

3. Chung, *Where the Wind Leads,* 204, and Chung, *Where the Wind Leads,* YouTube, May 7, 2014, https://www.youtube.com/watch ?v=j-e4qNfIbtg.

Chapter 10: A Purim People

1. Lorraine Boissoneault, "Why an Alabama Town Has a Monument Honoring the Most Destructive Pest in American History," *Smithsonian Magazine,* May 31, 2017, https://www.smithsonianmag. com/history/agricultural-pest-honored-herald-prosperity-enterprise -alabama-180963506/.

2. Yoram Hazony, *God and Politics in Esther* (New York: Cambridge University Press, 2016), 165.

3. Mike Cosper, *Faith Among the Faithless: Learning from Esther How to Live in a World Gone Mad* (Nashville, TN: Nelson, 2018), 167.

4. Cosper, *Faith Among the Faithless,* 167.

5. Kathy DeGagné, "Purim—A Story of Redemption," Bridges for Peace, January 10, 2013, https://www.bridgesforpeace.com/article/purima -story-of-redemption/.

6. Personal conversation with the author. Used by permission.

Chapter 11: You Were Made for This Moment

1. Fr. William Most, "Excerpts from St. Augustine," 1.4, EWTN, https://www.ewtn.com/catholicism/library/excerpts-from-st-augustine-9962.
2. Benjamin P. Browne, *Illustrations for Preaching* (Nashville, TN: Broadman, 1977), 72–73.

Questions for Reflection

1. Fr. William G. Most, "Excerpts from St. Augustine," 1.4, EWTN, https://www.ewtn.com/catholicism/library/excerpts-from-st-augustine-9962.

MAX LUCADO
BESTSELLERS

Anxious for Nothing

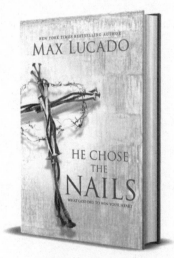

He Chose the Nails

Facing Your Giants

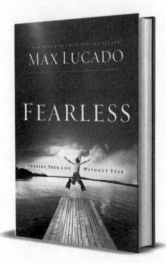

Fearless

WWW.MAXLUCADO.COM

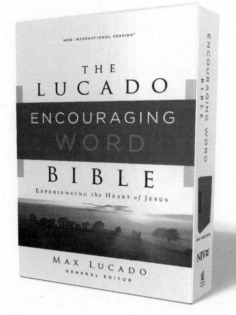

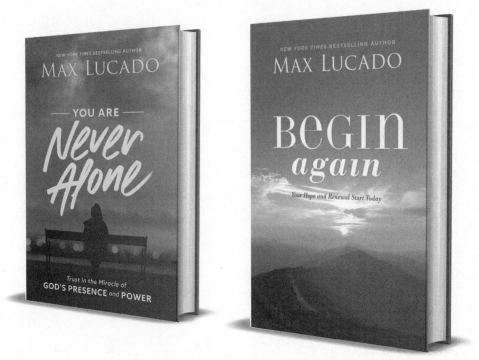

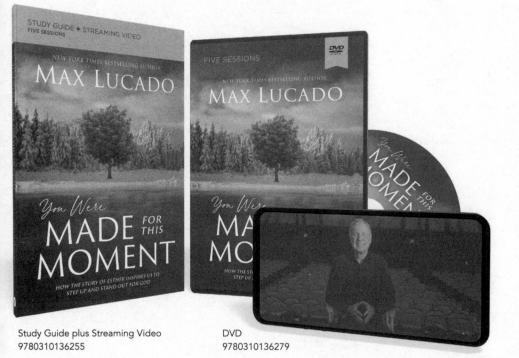